IDOLIZING PICTURES

THIS IS THE THIRTY-SECOND OF THE
WALTER NEURATH MEMORIAL LECTURES
WHICH ARE GIVEN ANNUALLY EACH SPRING ON
SUBJECTS REFLECTING THE INTERESTS OF
THE FOUNDER
OF THAMES & HUDSON

THE DIRECTORS
OF THAMES & HUDSON
WISH TO EXPRESS THEIR GRATITUDE
TO THE TRUSTEES OF
THE NATIONAL GALLERY, LONDON,
FOR GRACIOUSLY HOSTING
THESE LECTURES

IDOLIZING PICTURES

IDOLATRY, ICONOCLASM AND JEWISH ART

ANTHONY JULIUS

THAMES & HUDSON

The Walter Neurath Memorial Lectures, up to 1992, were given at Birkbeck College, University of London, whose Governors and Master most generously sponsored them for twenty-four years.

First published in the United States of America in paperback in 2001 by Thames & Hudson Inc., 500 Fifth Avenue, New York, New York 10110

Library of Congress Catalog Card Number 00-106214
ISBN 0-500-28262-5

Printed and bound in Italy by EBS

Idolizing Pictures *was written in a four-month period in early 2000. I began it in the weeks leading up to the trial of the libel action brought by the Holocaust denier David Irving against my client Deborah Lipstadt and her publishers, Penguin Books. The book was finished in the week that judgment was given. The judge concluded that Irving was a Holocaust denier, a falsifier of history, and an anti-Semite. Though Jews will thus always have to defend themselves against attacks from their enemies, there is a perception that anti-Semitism is in some sense constitutive of the Jewish experience. The view is that there are Jews because – some say, only because – there are anti-Semites. Though it has a Sartrean provenance, this belief has become part of the received wisdom on the subject of Jewish 'survival': without persecution, or the threat of persecution, the Jewish people would melt away. This view is, however, quite mistaken. Although I had several objects in writing this book, one was especially important to me. It was to affirm the vitality of the Jewish tradition, which does not depend upon anti-Semites to sustain it.*

The annual Walter Neurath Memorial Lecture was established by Thames & Hudson to honour its founder. He was, like so many others who have enriched the cultural life of this country, a victim of anti-Semitism. It was an honour to be invited to deliver the 2000 lecture, the origin of this book.

For Dina

Contents

1 Jean-Auguste-Dominique Ingres, *The Vow of Louis XIII*, 1824

THE WRITING OF THIS BOOK was prompted by my discovery of two pictures, Ingres' *The Vow of Louis XIII* (1824) and Komar and Melamid's *The Origins of Socialist Realism* (1982–83). Quite by chance, I came across them within a few weeks of each other. They are both about divinity, kingship and art. Ingres' work is a painting of God; Komar and Melamid's work is a painting of a man who claimed the authority of a god. Both pictures depict absolute rulers in communion with the divine. Louis experiences a vision of the Virgin and Child, while Stalin receives a visit from a Muse. *The Vow* declares its debt to Raphael, *The Origins* to Socialist Realism. While the parallels are thus quite striking, so are the contrasts. Ingres deals reverently with his subject, while Komar and Melamid are mockers. The vision is treated with awe; the visit is merely risible. Louis' Bourbon legitimacy is affirmed; Stalin's pretensions are exposed by being overstated. Raphael's mastery is celebrated; Socialist Realism's absurdity is punctured by being faithfully imitated.

The Vow was commissioned as an altarpiece for a cathedral and has an expressly Christian theme. In both subject and purpose it is thus a Christian art work, one in a long line of such art works that stretches back to 3rd-century sarcophagi and Roman catacomb paintings. This art confronted and resolved the following problem: if Christians were bound by the Mosaic prohibition against depicting God, how could they paint pictures of Christ? The answer that they gave to this question remains implicit in every work of Christian art painted since those early days. They said that the Incarnation mandated their art. If God acquired a human form, then that form must be capable of being depicted. He made Himself visible; art is a witness to that visibility. Christians had a duty to represent Christ, as an affirmation of the Incarnation. Their art is theology in a frame. So while the Mosaic prohibitions continued to apply, they no longer had the absolute and unqualified application that they had enjoyed hitherto. The implications of the Incarnation made for a massive exception, one which led to the translation of pagan art into a Christian vocabulary. The pagan Dionysus became the risen God; Minerva became Mary. For most Christians, Christian art makes neither false images of the true God nor images of false gods, but images of the true God. To a non-Christian (and indeed to some Christians), however, Christian art risks the idolatrous. As the non-Christian Ludwig Feuerbach put it in *The Essence of Christianity* (1841): 'The Son is the chief and ultimate principle of image-worship, for He is the image of God; and the image necessarily takes the place of the thing.'

The Origins was painted by two Russian Jews to be purchased by a private buyer or institution and to be displayed in a private space or museum. It is not a work of Christian art, though it draws on Byzantine iconography. It has no ecclesiastical function. Its mix of the pagan, the secular and the parodically Christian makes it hard to classify. I regard it as a Jewish work. It sets out to expose a false god, and confronts the challenge of the Mosaic prohibitions. It does so by its iconoclasm, conforming with the prohibitions by finding in them a positive mandate for its art. It thus does not rely upon the Incarnation to find for it an exception to the prohibitions; instead it affirms these prohibitions by its own idol-breaking projects. I believe this to be one of three specifically Jewish resolutions to the challenge of the prohibitions.

I will dwell on this Jewish resolution in part because the Christian one is so well established and successful. Christian art has resolved its relation to paganism; the old coin has been put to use again by being given a new stamp. What is more, Christian art continues to dominate the Western canon. Fully one third of the pictures in the National

2 Komar and Melamid, *The Origins of Socialist Realism*, 1982–83

Gallery are estimated by its director Neil MacGregor to be Christian, at least in the sense that they have a Christian subject. The fraction would be higher still if it included all those other, ostensibly non-Christian works nonetheless indebted to Christian iconography. Christian art is comfortable both in its relation to its predecessor, pagan art, and in its continued ascendancy in Western art as a whole. There is nothing, by contrast, that is comfortable about the Jewish resolution. It has yet adequately to be extrapolated from the actual artistic practices of Jewish artists; it has not yet provided the means by which a Jewish art may flourish. While Christian art has been held to have negotiated a space for itself distinct from the idolatrous, it is believed that Jewish art has largely failed to survive the destructive thrusts of the iconoclastic. The necessary precondition for Christian art – namely, a rejection of the Second Commandment – has been taken to be a precondition for art itself. I want to challenge these commonplaces, and to test the truth of the late Harold Rosenberg's remark that 'in regard to art, being Jewish appears to be no more than an accident' (an accident from which, presumably, the successful artist recovers).

Ingres / Komar and Melamid

In Ingres' *The Vow of Louis XIII*, the Catholic Louis is portrayed at the moment of solemnizing his vow as he dedicated France to the Virgin on the Feast of the Assumption in 1638. Ingres' huge work was commissioned in 1820 as an altarpiece for the cathedral at Montauban. It was exhibited at the 1824 Salon, where it was an enormous success, establishing Ingres as a painter of the first rank. He became the recognized leader of the conservative tendency.

The Vow combines two genres: history painting and religious painting. This merging of genres achieved a contemporary, secular objective: the sanctioning of the Restoration and of political reaction. The painting encourages a reverence for institutions and for the representatives of those institutions. By celebrating one monarch, it endorses another two. Ingres invests with the saintly authority of their Bourbon predecessor the worldly Louis XVIII and the brother who succeeded him in 1824, Charles X. The picture served as a rallying point for their adherents. Its setting in church made it the focus of religious devotion; its subject invited a comparable political deference. As an altarpiece, it would confront its audience with daunting authority.

The painting is structured as a hierarchy. The king is placed below the angels, who in turn defer to the Virgin. He is that paradox: sovereign, but subordinate. He lacks the imperial authority of the solitary figure in Ingres' *Napoleon I on his Imperial Throne* (1806); he has an independence denied to the supplicant in Ingres' *Jupiter and Thetis* (1811), draped submissively across the object of her prayers. Louis is presented in the

3 Jean-Auguste-Dominique Ingres, *Napoleon I on his Imperial Throne*, 1806

4 Jean-Auguste-Dominique Ingres, *Jupiter and Thetis*, 1811

5 *(left)* Raphael, *Crucifixion with Two Angels, the Virgin and Three Saints (the Mond Crucifixion)*, 1503–4
6 *(above)* Fra Bartolommeo, *Vision of Saint Bernard*, 1504–7

posture of a saint. Like the kneeling figures in Raphael's *Crucifixion with Two Angels, the Virgin and Three Saints (the Mond Crucifixion)* (1503–4) and Fra Bartolommeo's *Vision of Saint Bernard* (1504–7), anyone looking at the picture must stand at ground level and gaze upwards, as if in worship: in salon, church or museum the devotional posture is perhaps much the same. *The Vow* dwarfs its audience, who are situated as subjects of Monarch, Church and Artist.

The Montauban authorities had written to Ingres with instructions that the subject was to be Louis dedicating France to the Virgin on the Feast of the Assumption (which commemorates the day when, by Christian tradition, Mary died and was taken up, body and soul, to Heaven). Ingres misunderstood, and read the note as an instruction to do a picture of the king present at the Assumption itself. He wrote back, complaining that this was a hopeless anachronism. He thought, quite mistakenly, that these Church worthies wanted the Virgin present in the picture. His solution to this problem of his own invention was for her to be present, but as a vision. He would portray Louis experiencing a vision on the taking of his vow. The implication was that the vision was conferred on the king in acknowledgment of the sacred nature of his act.

The Montauban authorities accepted this solution and the Assumption was dropped. In his representation of the Virgin and Child Ingres borrowed from Raphael (as was his custom). This indebtedness of the picture to Raphael is not plagiarism but an open act of homage to a master of Christian iconography. Ingres' debt to Raphael was well known to his contemporaries; Baudelaire, for example, called him 'the artful adorer of Raphael' (*'l'adorateur rusé de Raphael'*). He first came into contact with Raphael's work as a young man in the Toulouse Académie, where he saw a copy of the *Madonna and Child with Saint John (Madonna della Sedia)* (1513). He drew on aspects of this work in many of his own pictures, sometimes incorporating it in miniature as a signature. It appears, for example, painted into the carpet in *Napoleon* (1806). Copying Raphael was for Ingres a badge of his own originality. And motherhood, usually without any accompanying infant, was a theme to which Ingres returned repeatedly in his career. As one art book puts it, Raphael was his 'idol'.

7 Raphael, *Madonna and Child with Saint John (Madonna della Sedia)*, 1513

The picture is thus both about Louis' devotion to Virgin and Child and Ingres' devotion to Raphael. They overlap: on Raphael's death the artist was compared to Jesus, and given the fictional age of 33 to make a unity of his death and Christ's. And while Ingres' adoration of his predecessor-artist thus acquires a religious hue, Louis' adoration of the Virgin takes on an aesthetic colouring if we regard him as the artist's proxy, worshipping not the Virgin herself, or even her image, but an art work. Ingres has Louis kneel before the work of Raphael. There is thus no tension here between a devotion to art and all its possibilities, and a devotion to the State and all its demands. In this work, indeed, the two become aspects of each other. Raphael *is* Art; Louis *is* the State. And the picture's audience is positioned, supine, beneath both.

There is a certain innocence about this; it is perhaps the last moment in history that such an affirmation could be made without complication or elaborate self-justification. Certainly, just fifteen years later, Théophile Gautier was writing: 'I should most joyfully renounce my rights as a Frenchman and as a citizen to see an authentic picture by Raphael.' Only a little while before, a writer or artist could have both. Indeed, Louis XIII – exemplary Frenchman and artist-proxy – is granted by Ingres a vision of Raphael. For Ingres himself, *The Vow*, with its representation of a Raphael, was itself an affirmation of French citizenship. It is a picture which attests to the artist's commitment to throne and altar; in the year that it was exhibited, Ingres returned to France from Italy, where he had lived for eighteen years. Ingres' work was created in the last moment before Gautier formulated his challenge to artists and writers: art, or the State?

The Vow thus has a worshipper and an object of worship. Depending on how one reads the work, the worshipper is the king, or the artist, or the king as artist. And the object of worship is either the Virgin (as vision or image), or Raphael's art – perhaps art itself. Whichever one chooses, however, the relation between the two sides is a constant. It has three features: subordination, reverence and the attributing of divine powers. The worshipper defers to the object of his worship. Indeed, to some extent at least, the deference contributes to his very identity. This deference is not forced, nor is it resented. It is freely given in acknowledgment of the overwhelming authority of the object of worship, which has the power to intervene in the worshipper's life and change it for the better.

Ingres' picture is not a study of idolatry – unlike, for example, Raphael's *Adoration of the Golden Calf* (1516–19). It is not a visual inquiry into idolatry; it does not take idolatry as its subject. But although it is thus not itself reflective, it takes us to the brink of thought. It is, one might say, maximally *un*reflective (I borrow the phrase from Charles Taylor's account of Hegel's aesthetics). By the complexity of its representation, it makes reflection unavoidable. The picture poses the problem of idolatry in its uncritical deference to the continuing authority of the

8 Raphael, *Adoration of the Golden Calf*, 1516–19

9 David Allan, *The Origin of Painting*, 1775

10 Luca Cambiaso, *Madonna and Child*, *c.* 1565

Virgin, Raphael, and the Bourbon monarchy. Ingres kneels, and invites his audience to kneel, before the symbols of religion, art and state.

I now pass from the official art of the French Restoration to the *Un*official Art of the Soviet Union, so called because it subsisted, in some danger, without State approval. Komar and Melamid's *The Origins of Socialist Realism* (fig. 2) shows Joseph Stalin relaxed yet alert, receiving a visit from the Muse of painting. With her left hand, she traces Stalin's profile, thereby creating the first Socialist Realist picture. Komar and Melamid allude, jokingly, to the legend related by Pliny in which a young Corinthian woman, dismayed at her lover's imminent departure, draws his image to console herself during his absence and thereby invents the art of portraiture. This primal scene was at one time a popular subject for artists: see, for example, David Allan's *The Origin of Painting* (1775). With her right hand, the Muse caresses Stalin's chin, a gesture of similarly dense iconographic significance. It was with a 'chin chuck' that the Christ child typically expressed his relation to the Virgin: see, for example, Luca Cambiaso's *Madonna and Child* (*c.* 1565).

In contrast to *The Vow*, *The Origins* was *not* a commissioned work. It was *not* exhibited at a Salon. It was *not* received with acclaim in Russia. It has a secular and pagan subject, *not* a religious one. Each work thus possesses qualities the other excludes. But there is more than this to the relation between the two; the bonds are more intimate. *The Origins* recapitulates *The Vow*, but in the key of irony. The one is a negative imprint of the other.

Vitaly Komar and Alexander Melamid started collaborating in 1972, and now work together in New York. Sotsart, a word made up of the first syllable of Socialist Realism and the last syllable of Pop Art, was their invention. Sotsart differs from Pop Art partly because it takes an art form rather than cultural artifacts as its subject, and partly because it lacks Pop Art's ambivalence. Sotsart finds nothing whatever to celebrate in Socialist Realism; Pop Art takes a certain delight in representing just what it is that makes today's homes so different, so appealing. In this respect, Pop Art is closer to Socialist Realism itself than to its ironic restatement, Sotsart. Sotsart blinks with mock perplexity at just what it was that made Stalin so different, so appalling. It is, in Ekaterina Andreeva's phrase, a series of games played against idols. *The Origins* is an exemplary Sotsart work.

Socialist Realism was a style of art legislated by the Soviet State. It emerged in the late 1920s, and was confirmed in 1934 as the only acceptable kind of painting. The immediate object of State attention was literature; art followed in its wake. It was not Stalin himself who originated it (he wasn't much interested in art, unlike Hitler). Indeed, it marks a regression to the iconic art of Byzantium. The General Secretary is divine; Central Committee members are saints or disciples. The expressionless stares invited audiences to become inward with the ideals of Communism. The 17th-century tradition of 'parsuny' (portraits of the living as if icons), the gradual emergence in the following centuries of an academic art of portraiture – it was as if none of this had happened. Mikhail Roshal's *We Shall Mine Extra Coal* (1973) mocks just

11 Mikhail Roshal, *We Shall Mine Extra Coal*, 1973

this willed art-historical amnesia. Both Socialist Realism and Sotsart have a relation to Christian art: the former in unconscious mimicry; the latter in conscious irony.

According to its foremost English student, Matthew Cullerne Bown, Socialist Realism had three objectives: the representation of Soviet life; the glorification of the Revolution; and the communication of the ideals of Communism. These restate the principal themes of Christian art: representations from Christ's ministry; the glorification of his death; and the communication of the ideals of Christianity. Socialist Realism promotes a rival religion. 'Only the art of Socialist Realism is legitimate,' announced a party ideologist, 'it reflects a truthful world-view, and expresses the beautiful in art.' Its prescriptions, in themselves absurd and repressive, quickly degenerated into (or perhaps I should say found their proper level in) mostly fictitious representations of Stalin's life; glorifications of his leadership; and the communication of his doctrines. Socialist Realism has its place at the terminal point in the

12 Komar and Melamid, *Double Self-Portrait as Young Pioneers*, 1983

long decline of Socialism across the last century, as it withered from a theory of political liberation into a spirit-enervating idolatry. Socialism became a theory of Stalin's perfection, Socialist Realism the visual form of this theory.

It is at this point that the correspondences between the Ingres work and the Komar and Melamid work end. Both are estimable, even important works of art. But unlike *The Vow*, *The Origins* is reflective. It is both a picture and a meta-picture. It is the work's irony that gives it this double existence. Irony is the work's passport, so speak, to the realm of philosophy which is, by its nature, iconoclastic (all that philosophy can do, said Wittgenstein, is to destroy idols). Ingres was a great painter; Komar and Melamid are both great painters and great thinkers about painting.

Sotsart articulates the official truth of the Soviet regime, but with a literalist enthusiasm that jars. In its ironic over-eagerness, it undermines what it purportedly celebrates. It is a kind of derisive applause. Thinking one time about its implications, I remembered an incident from my school days. It was the end of the summer term and an unloved and brutal teacher was retiring after forty or more years of service. At the final school assembly, the headmaster sent him off with a warm speech, and invited the school to show its appreciation by applause. This began in a perfunctory, half-hearted way; in response to the headmaster's frowns it swelled grudgingly. But then it became intense and prolonged. Cheers broke out. Why? Because we had discovered irony. In the end, the headmaster put a stop to the applause, its mocking purpose impossible to ignore. This was irony by overpraise. Komar and Melamid's *Double Self-Portrait as Young Pioneers* (1983) does the same: it opposes by extravagantly endorsing; dissents by the comical vigour of its support.

The Origins thus exploits the clichés of Socialist Realism, Stalin's pose and visionary stare familiar from endless works of the period: see, for example, Feodor Shurpin's *The Morning of Our Fatherland* (1948) and Sergei Merkurov's *Joseph Stalin* (1940s). Komar and Melamid turn the style against itself, and thereby demonstrate that art will always have

13 Feodor Shurpin, *The Morning of Our Fatherland*, 1948
14 Sergei Merkurov, *Joseph Stalin*, 1940s

the capacity (if not the desire) to elude the prescriptions of the State. Even the most conservative style can be subverted – that is to say, adapted for ends contrary to those that it intends to promote. Komar and Melamid turn idols into figures of fun.

Idolatry

What then is meant by idolatry? No one admits to being an idol worshipper. To describe a practice as idolatrous is to take for granted its wrong-headedness: it is primitive, misconceived and shaming. Primitive, because it is to be associated with the earliest stages of religious belief – with the Canaanites and all those other scriptural adversaries of the Jews. Misconceived, because the idol worshipper in his devotions has mistaken the merely human or material for the divine. Shaming, because this worship is marked by an uncritical subordination by a person to a mere object, a submissiveness which lacks all dignity and sense. The idolator demands help from the idol. He displays a misplaced and absurd intensity of feeling towards it. In his folly, he worships the work of his own hands, that which his own fingers have made (Isaiah, 3:8). That dead matter rules the quick, says Cynthia Ozick, is the law of idolatry.

The idolator seeks to eliminate from his consciousness all awareness of the materiality of his idol. And the competent idol maker will do everything he can to ensure that his customers are not distracted by the idol's design or 'finish': he carves an object out of wood so that others may see a god. There is an echo of precisely this objective in Ingres' defence of the *fini* (the finished texture of the art work, the 'licked surface'): 'The brush stroke, as accomplished as it may be, should not be visible: otherwise it prevents the illusion, immobilizes everything. Instead of the object represented, it calls attention to the process: instead of the thought it betrays the hand.'

Any misplaced reverence can be dismissed as idolatry, which may therefore be expanded to include the willing, uncritical subordination of one person to another (provided, of course, that the subordination does not possess the mandate of truth). Luther, for example, considered idolatrous any appeals for help or comfort directed anywhere other than to God. This includes, he added, the seeking of help or comfort from one's own works. To do this is to attempt to 'force God to yield his Heaven'. If you do not defer to God, you will find yourself deferring to an idol. As Eusebius put it, 'God is not pleased by what he himself did not produce.... Those things which are not of God must be of his rival.'

Idolatry is thus a term which can only be accompanied by verbs in the second or third person. *I* worship the true god or gods; *you* are an idol worshipper. *I* am a properly sceptical person, mindful of my standing as a rational, thinking agent; *you* are a gullible, weak-minded ninny, in thrall to the false charisma of another person, or to the false magic of 'silver and gold, the work of men's hands' (Psalms, 115:4). *My* discriminating perspectives are a credit to my independence of mind; *your* unqualified fidelity is a betrayal of your reason.

This castigating of idolatry developed over time into a theory of ideology. It is possible to identify the stages of this transformation. First, there was the Protestant critique of Catholicism ('no images, no Papists' the Canterbury crowds chanted in 1640). Then there was the Enlightenment critique of revealed religion. A critique of folk religion became a critique of religion in general. All prayer, wherever and however directed, is idolatrous if the object of prayer is a mere invention of the worshipper. An idolator then becomes any person alienated from the sources of his creativity. He does not recognize what he worships to be his own work. This mystification is what is now called false consciousness, and represents perhaps the only durable contribution of Marxism to the social sciences. The theory of ideology broadens and secularizes the category of idols, but it maintains the distinction between idol and idolator. There is one further stage. Beyond the theory of ideology lies an anthropology – a theory of man – which holds that the idolator is himself a construction of the idol. He is realized in his idolatry. Human beings, that is, are mere instantiations of ideology. The very notion of the 'human' is an ideological figure. This anthropology thus collapses into its opposite, as it returns to the idol the creative mastery that the theories of idolatry and ideology denied it. There is thus no liberation for the idolator; the most that can be won is a knowledge of the laws of one's slavery (I quote from Louis Althusser). It is a bleak terminus.

Idolatry of the State, idolatry of art: these are the commonest forms taken by modern idolatry. The art work and the State become idols, alienated from their makers and given a false sovereignty.

While Russian and German artists have reflected this political idolatry (see, for example, Otto Hoyer's blasphemous *In the Beginning Was the Word* of 1937), Russian and German intellectuals have had the greatest cause to reflect upon it. This is Karl Barth on National Socialism: 'We were in danger of bringing, first incense, and then the complete sacrifice to it as a false god.' And Paul Tillich: 'Idolatry is the elevation of a preliminary concern to ultimacy ... something essentially

15 Otto Hoyer, *In the Beginning Was the Word*, 1937

finite is given infinite significance (the best example of contemporary idolatry is religious nationalism).' In his last work, completed in America in the final year of World War II, Ernst Cassirer proposed that of all human idols, the political idols are the most dangerous and the most enduring. They defeat rational thought and promote forms of worship that are pernicious in their effects. They blind their adherents, and do far worse to their adherents' enemies.

As for idolatry of art, consider this poem, written in 1899 in Odessa by the Hebrew poet Saul Tchernichovski. He apostrophizes Apollo: 'I come to thee and bow before thine image, / Thine image-symbol of the light in life: / I prostrate myself to the exalted and the good, / To things of high estate upon the earth, / To all majestic in creation's bounds, / To all the highest mysteries of art...'. He rather overdoes it, of course. This setting out to affront Jewish sensibilities with exaggerated, almost absurd gestures doesn't fool anyone. More idolatrous than the idolators – a parody of an idolator, even – his transports of worship are intended for an audience composed exclusively of co-religionists. He addresses Apollo, but he speaks to Jews. And he gives witness to the Jewish revulsion at idolatry, and the prohibition of images, by the very theatricality of his dithyrambs. A whole culture of idol-breaking is evoked – in relief, so to speak – by these lines. It is a Jewish culture; at one time it was a Christian culture too. And then things changed and Christians had to confront the challenge of art.

The Christian resolution

The early Church Fathers forbade images. In *The City of God* (completed 426) Augustine held that 'the one God should be worshipped without an image.' This was in accordance with the worship of the first Christians. They were poor, and could not afford images; they were persecuted, and did not want to draw attention to themselves; as former Jews, they were in the habit of taking seriously the Second Commandment; as former pagans, they were heirs to a certain cultivated, Graeco-Roman contempt for idolatry; while paganism itself persisted, Christians were keen to distinguish their practices from pagan ones.

All of this encouraged the artist-writers of the Italian Renaissance to regard the early Christian Church as uniformly iconoclastic and anti-art. Lorenzo Ghiberti (1378–1455), for example, claimed that all the statues and paintings of antiquity had been destroyed, and along with them, the theoretical writings and the rules for teaching these arts. The Church whitewashed the temples, he said, and punished painters and sculptors, all just to persecute idolators. Art was brought to an end.

But Ghiberti radically overstated his case. There was some breaking of pagan statues by Christians, especially during Constantine's reign, but most survived (many to decorate Constantine's new capital). The Church embraced images quite early on in its history. Since God realized Himself as a man, His depiction must be possible: Word becomes flesh becomes image. As Hegel remarked, art provides Christianity with the means by which 'the actual appearance of God, which has passed away, is perpetually repeated and renewed.' Christians need art; it keeps the faithful alert to the mysteries of faith. According to Christian tradition, Saint Luke himself was a painter – the 'first Christian painter' said the 14th-century Italian Cennino Cennini. Luke became the patron saint of painters. They continue his holy work and are thus subject to the direction of the Church. For example, the encyclical *Mediator Dei*, issued by Pope Pius XII in 1947, stipulates: 'It is absolutely necessary that all men should individually come into vital contact with the Sacrifice of the Cross ... [the modern artist] wanders from the right path ... who commands that images of our Divine Redeemer on the Cross be so made that His body does not show the bitter wounds that He suffered.'

Given the theological significance of art to Christianity, it is not surprising that debates over its permissible limits were especially bloody and destructive. Such, for example, was the Byzantine iconoclastic controversy of the 8th century. The iconoclasts contended for the continuing authority of the Mosaic prohibitions; the iconodules maintained that these prohibitions must give way before the greater authority of the Incarnation. Indeed, to deny that Christ was capable of being portrayed was to deny the Incarnation itself. In such a context, it was an easy thing to dismiss the Second Commandment. John of Damascus, the 8th-century iconophile, wrote: 'These injunctions [against idols] were given to the Jews on account of their proneness to idolatry. We, on the contrary are no longer children.... When he who is without form ... takes upon himself the form of a servant ... you may draw his likeness and show it to anyone willing to contemplate it.' Even his opponents, however, did not object to pictures of the human form (the iconoclastic emperors put their own images on coins).

The Byzantine iconoclasts attempted to return Christianity to the purity of its first devotions, and the rigour of its early repudiation of paganism. Was it not obvious, they complained, that images of Christ on his judgment throne derived from images of Zeus, and that images of the Virgin succeeded images of pagan mother-goddesses? But the attempt failed. The iconodules, their antagonists, argued that an image could not be confused with the original. It was patently an imitation. John of Damascus made the nice distinction: 'Christ is venerated not *in* the image but *with* the image.' The iconodules were rather good at making such distinctions, while there was a certain lack of intellectual sophistication about the iconoclasts. These image-breakers were also constrained by their Christian faith; they had to concede the Incarnation, which meant that Jesus was a bridge, or mediator, between the human and divine. The iconodules persuasively argued that the icon served a related purpose, and that their opponents' hostility to images was equivalent to hostility to Christ himself. An illustration in the 9th-century Chludov Psalter depicts iconoclasts as continuing the work of the soldiers who tormented Christ on the cross. Pope Gregory I

16 The Crucifixion and iconoclasts, from the Chludov Psalter, *c.* 850–75

explained to an iconoclastic bishop: 'You … should have both preserved the images and prohibited the people from adoring them.' This inability to discriminate, a consequence of the combination of the crude and the compromised in the iconoclasts' thinking, meant that in the main iconoclasm expressed itself in violent action rather than considered argument. The contest between these Christian adversaries was (as one historian of the period describes it) a feud and not just a controversy. It was not mere polemical strife but actual war declared by one part of Christendom against the other.

The dispute did not settle the question for good. Sometimes, for short periods, iconoclasts prevailed. But until the Reformation, on each occasion that they pressed their arguments, they were defeated by a combination of force and logic – the institutional force of the Church, and the theological logic of the Incarnation. It remains the case that there is no single course taken by Christianity regarding images of the divine. Calvinism, in its insistent iconophobia, is the most faithful to the prohibitions. The art of the Italian Renaissance did not flinch from portraying the Father as well as the Son, which surely went beyond the mandate for art provided by the doctrine of the Incarnation: see, for example, Masaccio's *The Trinity* (*c.* 1427). This art was part of a culture in which images were treated, as one historian of the period puts it, as powerful objects which could be used to intercede with God. Russian Orthodoxy, in its reverence of the icon, takes to their furthest extent the implications for art of the Incarnation. The icon manifests its prototype. It thus must be worshipped and has the ability to work miracles. The icon embodies, it has been said, 'spiritual, sacred, corporeity'. It is more than art; it is a means by which one may apprehend the divine. Icons are *acheiropoieta* ('things made without hands'), that is to say, precisely *not* the idols mocked by the Prophets. Ingres' *The Vow* may be situated on an arc described between these two extremes, though at some distance from the iconophobic end (altar art was a particular target of Reformation iconoclasts).

17 Masaccio,
The Trinity, c. 1427

Though Jews did not participate in these Christian image-wars, reference was made to them by both sides. The iconodules were accused of being no better than Jews, inveterate idolators. The iconoclasts were accused of being no better than Jews, deniers of the Incarnation. Whatever else they disagreed about, the two sides could therefore unite on their common hostility to the Jews. In the early Church, it was the received wisdom that the Jews had sinned against God by their idolatrous practices; to the medieval Church, any attack on the worship of images was the work of 'judaizing' heretics. It is to Judaism proper that I now turn.

The Jewish resolution

It is sometimes said that the difference between Judaism and Christianity is that while the Jews are still waiting for the Messiah, the Christians believe that He arrived two thousand years ago. But this is to misunderstand the quite different notions of the messianic in the two religions. Judaism does not contemplate the enfleshment of God. Jews do not expect Him ever to walk among his creation; they have not deferred their figurative art to the moment of His arrival. 'Let no one think,' wrote Maimonides, 'that in the days of the Messiah anything of the natural course of the world will cease or that any innovation will be introduced into creation. Rather, the world will continue in its accustomed course.'

God, said Franz Rosenzweig, had to found a religion, *which is but an anti-religion*, in order to combat the 'religionitis' of mankind. Judaism depopulates the heavens. During the 1st century CE, Alexandria experienced an influx of Jewish messianic revolutionaries from Palestine. The destruction of pagan temples, the historian John Gager has written, was part of their messianic campaign. These assaults on religious sites gave rise in turn to the widespread use of the phrase 'impious Jews'. It is Judaism as 'anti-religion' to which the art of Komar and Melamid precisely answers, and they are just such impious Jews. Their art is a Jewish art, one which is derived from a Jewish aesthetics.

Referring to Lenin's embalmed body in the mausoleum at the heart of Soviet culture, they remark that 'it was hard to be Jews in the land of mummies and pyramids.' They mean a land of idols and the worship of the dead. That Komar and Melamid are Jewish is a fact about them that I want to take seriously, for a number of reasons. Partly, because it is always interesting when Jews become artists, given the conventional wisdom that they are not cut out for it; partly because there were very few Jewish artists before the middle of the 19th century, and then suddenly there were a number, and it is interesting to ask why; but principally – and this is the main burden of my argument – because there is a connection to be made between the painterly irony I have just been talking about and what we might term Jewish aesthetics.

The principles of Jewish aesthetics are cast in negative terms. The prohibition against idol-worshipping may be found first in Exodus and then again in Deuteronomy. This is the relevant passage from Exodus 20:

> 3. Thou shalt have no other gods before me.
> 4. Thou shalt not make unto thee any graven image, or any likeness of any thing that is in heaven above, or that is in the earth beneath, or that is in the water under the earth:
> 5. Thou shalt not bow down thyself to them, nor serve them: for I the Lord thy God am a jealous God...

These prohibitions are then restated, in an elaborated and admonitory form, in Deuteronomy 4:

> 15. Take ye therefore good heed unto yourselves: for ye saw no manner of similitude on the day that the Lord spake unto you in Horeb out of the midst of the fire:
> 16. Lest ye corrupt yourselves, and make you a graven image, the similitude of any figure, the likeness of any male or female,

17. The likeness of any beast that is on the earth, the likeness of any winged fowl that flieth in the air,
18. The likeness of any thing that creepeth on the ground, the likeness of any fish that is in the waters beneath the earth:
19. And lest thou lift up thine eyes unto heaven and when thou seest the sun, and the moon, and the stars, even all the host of heaven, shouldest be driven to worship them, and serve them...
...
23. Take heed unto yourselves, lest ye forget the covenant of the Lord your God, which he made with you, and make you a graven image, or the likeness of any thing, which the Lord thy God hath forbidden thee.
24. When thou shalt beget children, and children's children, and ye shall have remained long in the land, and shall corrupt yourselves, and make a graven image, or the likeness of any thing, and shall do evil in the sight of the Lord thy God and provoke him to anger...

This adds to Exodus, mainly by giving reasons for the prohibitions: God is incorporeal and therefore cannot be represented; there is a risk that sculpted figures will become objects of worship. Images of God are banned because they can never capture His likeness, and it would be a presumption even to try (call this 'the first prohibition'). Images of the living and of the planets are banned because of the risk that they may promote idolatry (call this 'the second prohibition'). As the 1st-century Jewish historian Josephus put it: 'all materials, let them be ever so costly, are unworthy to compose an image for him, and all arts are unartful to express the notion we ought to have of him.' 'Our legislator,' he adds, 'has forbidden us to make images ... for fear that any be worshipped as gods.'

Images are one thing, words are quite another. In the Jewish tradition, language made the world. God can be represented in language, because unlike art, language can render absence, and has the ability to point beyond its own limits (the inexpressible, the infinite, etc.). And again unlike art, it does not allow any blurring of the representation and the thing represented, the signifier and the signified; while one cannot take words for things, one can be deceived into confusing pictures of things with the things themselves. Language has art at a double disadvantage. The aural is thus superior to the visual. 'Paganism sees its gods,' remarked the Jewish historian Heinrich Graetz, 'Judaism hears Him.'

The prohibition against images insists upon a radical divide between God and His creation. It is because idolatry seeks to bridge that divide that the Talmud regards it as one of the sins that must be resisted even on pain of death. 'There is nothing that the Halakhah [i.e., Jewish law] loathes and despises as much,' says the modern Rabbinical sage J.B. Soloveitchik, 'as the idea of cultic mediation or the choosing of individuals, on the basis of supernatural considerations, to be intercessors for the community.' Maimonides holds that the laws against idolatry are the source of all other prohibitions. He says that the principal purpose of the Law was the removal and utter destruction of idolatry. It is only in relation to idolatry that one finds reference in the Scriptures to God's 'jealousy', and none but the idolator is called 'enemy' or 'hater of the Lord'. To repudiate idolatry is thus to be faithful to the whole Torah. According to R. Israel of Rizhin, the messianic world will be one entirely cleansed of images. It will be a world 'in which the image and its object can no longer be related.' Existence will elude representation, and idolatry will be impossible.

None of this means, of course, that Jewish culture has found no room for art. On the contrary, art has a very specific, prescribed place. An ornamental or decorative art is expressly sanctioned by the Scriptures and derives from the verse, 'this is my God and I will adorn him' (Exodus 15:2). Exodus tells the story of the craftsman Bezalel's role in the construction and decoration of the Tabernacle. He is praised for his wisdom and his piety, as well as for his skill 'in all manner of workmanship'. He has the ability to 'devise curious works, to work in gold, and in silver, and in the cutting of stones ... and in carving wood, to make any manner of cunning work' (35:32–3). The ark he creates has golden cherubim, vessels, candlesticks, bowls and lamps. This is a craftsmanship which is subordinate to religious observance. The very materials that the craftsman works upon are sanctified by the use to which they are put. By adorning a place of worship they are in some sense being returned to God. This idea of craftsmanship does not therefore inhibit a general disparagement of the visual arts. Art, a Jewish sage once wrote, 'ascends from sensuous objects to the gods'. It is the antithesis of prophetic monotheism.

The anecdotal evidence of Jewish mistrust of art is quite strong. The American artist Maurice Sterne recalled that as a child living in a small Russian town he had been punished by his Rabbi for drawing a picture of the man on the ground with a stick. A great uncle of Chagall is said to have refused to give his hand to his young nephew on learning that he drew. Earlier in that century, a young sculptor, Joseph Engel, was instructed by his Rabbi to mutilate all the human faces that he had sculpted. Art was for many centuries a stranger to Jews, a Jewish critic once remarked (and an unwelcome one at that). Stories of this kind typify the reception of Jewish artists in their own communities (they have even been the basis of novels – see Chaim Potok's *My Name is Asher Lev* [New York, 1972]). And implicated in these stories is a mistrust of Christianity.

In essence, the prohibitions refuse to distinguish between the three terms in the series: idol, icon, image. That is to say, Judaism collapses the second and the third term into the first; icons and images are, or have the capacity to become, idols. The innocent image is ever at risk of turning into the illegitimate idol. There can be no idolatry without images. Christianity, by contrast, must insist upon the distinctness of each of the three, rejecting the idol, embracing the icon, and admitting the image.

There are two readings of the prohibitions, the 'literal' and the 'liberal'. The literal reading paraphrases Exodus; the liberal reading interprets Deuteronomy. The literal reading asserts that certain images are forbidden; the liberal reading adds, where the object is idolatry. Jewish history discloses an almost unqualified fidelity to the prohibition against picturing God, but only an incomplete and intermittent conformity with the prohibition against depicting God's creation. This latter laxity has been justified by reliance on the liberal reading. So while the literal reading has simplicity and certainty on its side, the liberal reading has history on *its* side. Indeed, the very reason for its existence is precisely to reconcile proscription and history. And since the Talmud declares that idolatry has been abolished (*Avodah Zara* 17a-b), it may be relied upon to justify practically any image whatsoever. The second prohibition can almost disappear in the liberal reading, which thus operates as a kind of erasure.

The received view of the prohibitions is that they are at best merely permissive of certain types of art enterprise. No general theory of art may be derived from them. They allow, they do not enable. They sieve art, excluding certain images, allowing others. They subtract proscribed representations from a notional sum of representations available to artists. This proscriptive understanding of the prohibitions is common to both the literal and the liberal reading. They differ only to the extent of what they would forbid. The liberal reading would subtract scenes of Christ's life and death, and representations of God. The literal reading would subtract rather more. But the readings do operate in much the same manner. And what remains after they have done their work is what then becomes available to Jewish artists.

'We all know,' remarks a Jewish art critic, 'that religious injunctions impaired the early development of visual arts.' He stresses 'early'. The good news, apparently, is that in the last hundred years Jewish art has found a way past the prohibitions. Through happy coincidence, and by a development in art which has nothing to do with the prohibitions themselves, the Jewish artist is no longer excluded from the artistic practices of his or her contemporaries. Abstract art is non-figurative; Cubist and post-Cubist art distorts the human form. Modern art, this argu-

18 Kazimir Malevich, *Black Square*, 1915

ment goes, has at last caught up with the prohibitions. It is correctly described, and correctly condemned, by reference to their fiat: correctly described, because of the ostensible aniconicism of the art of the first half, and the partial iconoclasm of the second half, of the century; correctly condemned, because of the unqualifiedly idolatrous art of the totalitarian mid-century. Indeed, some enthusiasts have even gone so far as to propose that the art of the 20th century is thus essentially 'Jewish'. Others, not quite so extravagant, have averred that at the very least modern art is 'right up [the Jewish artist's] street'.

This is an attractive position to take, and so it is unfortunate that it is misconceived. It cannot explain why, if abstract art is so congenial to Jews, so many modern Jewish artists eschewed the abstract in favour of the figurative – consider the careers of Chagall, Soutine, Modigliani, Kitaj. The significance of the roughly coincident arrival in the art world of abstract art and the major modern Jewish artists has been overstated. When Adorno writes that abstract art has 'something of the old prohibitions of graven images' about it, he is being lazy. The advent of abstract art had much more to do with a certain diffuse Christian spirituality than

19 ‘0.10’ exhibition, Petrograd 1915–16

with the precepts of Jewish law (see, for example, the writings of Kandinsky). And hidden within the abstract was a new iconicism.

Consider Malevich’s *From Cubism to Suprematism: The New Painterly Realism* (1915), and his *Black Square* (1915). In polemic and painting, Malevich both repudiates and lets back in the iconic. A gesture of abolition is followed by a cancelling gesture of reincorporation. The violence of his language, his iconoclastic fury at the figurative, the square as if blanking it out, or barring its very possibility, is provoked by outrage at its demeaning of the artist. The representational diminishes the artist, who is a creator. His work is analogous to God’s. And then, almost at the end of the polemic, and implicit in the painting, Malevich announces: ‘the square is a living, regal infant’. The allusion is unmistakable: it is the infant Christ that Malevich finds in the square. At the ‘0.10’ exhibition in Petrograd, it hung just under the ceiling, across the two walls, where icons are traditionally hung in Russian homes. Malevich thus travels the greatest possible distance from the figurative in order to reinvent the iconic.

There thus seems to be a gap between the practices of most Jewish artists and the prohibitions, which have been frequently disregarded as an obstacle to creativity. That gap cannot be bridged by any opportunistic promoting of abstract art or Cubist art as Jewish art practices. The abstract aesthetic is not a Jewish one. But that does not mean that it cannot be bridged at all. There is a connection, and it can be made (that is, disclosed) by a reading of the Second Commandment which, in contrast to both the literal and liberal readings, finds in it the positive obligation to combat idolatry. The Second Commandment does not (or does not just) inhibit; it mobilizes. It enlists Jews in a project of idol-breaking. This project has an aesthetic dimension; it can be given artistic expression. Given this gloss, the Second Commandment opens out onto a complex range of artistic possibilities. While it is, in its familiar guise, a proscriptive jurisprudence, it is also an empowering aesthetics, though of a uniquely difficult kind. It mandates three kinds of visual art.

There is, first, an art of the infinite, the unbounded, the sublime. I derive this from the first prohibition, and will call it 'aniconic art'. It is art's response to language's challenge, its attempt to vindicate the tag *ut pictura poesis* by matching language's powers. It seeks to abolish the icon and thereby remove the double disadvantage that language puts it under. One might think that art is limited to rendering what is finite and present. Aniconic art seeks to render the infinite and to put presence in question.

Second, there is an art of ornament, illustration or witness. I derive this from the second prohibition, and will call it 'iconic art'. It is the art most rooted in scriptural sanction and historical experience, and constitutes the default, as it were, of the Jewish artist. It is the most obvious, and therefore the most travelled, route to Jewish content. (Anyone familiar with examples of this art is likely to conclude that in many cases, the journey should not have been made.) It domesticates the icon, making it serve a larger Jewish purpose: decorating a synagogue wall, beautifying a ritual, honouring a religious sage or political leader, bearing witness to the material or spiritual aspects of Jewish communal life.

And third, there is an art of idol-breaking, which I also derive from the second prohibition, and which I will call 'iconoclastic art'. It attacks the icon. It is to be distinguished from the iconoclasm of avant-garde art, which attacks conformist or academic art merely as a means of self-definition. Idol-breaking iconoclasm is serious; avant-garde art often is not. The one posits a world without idols; the other often merely seeks to replace one idol with another (itself).

These three are all derived from the prohibitions. Each one contests the authority of the idol. The aniconic disregards it, the iconic demotes it, the iconoclastic subverts or breaks it. For as long as idolatry persists, there will be a need for all three kinds of Jewish art.

Jewish aniconicism

Three of the leading Abstract Expressionists were Jewish by origin: Barnett Newman, Mark Rothko and Adolph Gottlieb. Some enthusiasts of their work have taken this as their cue to find a Jewish quality in their work. The quality they have found is one of sublimity, which they relate to the first prohibition. Avram Kampf, the author of *Chagall to Kitaj: Jewish Experience in 20th-Century Art* (London, 1990), writes: 'Newman worked in the classic "no graven image" tradition of Judaism not because images are forbidden, but because the absolute cannot be rendered by an image. It is a purely abstract conception, imageless, like the Jewish God.' And then he adds: 'If there were a Jewish style, Newman's work would be regarded as its most authentic and classic expression.'

This is not an altogether misplaced enthusiasm. Or if it is, it is one shared by a number of critics who would not be led there by any inclination to talk up Jewish art. Kant, for example, acknowledges the prohibitions in one of the passages on the sublime in his *Critique of Judgment* (1790). The experience of the sublime, he explains, is one of the thrusting aside of the barriers of the sensible world. It is a presentation of the infinite. It expands the soul. And then he goes on: 'Perhaps there is no more sublime passage in the Jewish Law than the commandment: Thou shalt not make unto thee any graven image....'

This negative presentation of the Divine, he says, is a remedy against fanaticism. Fanatics look for visions; they want to see beyond the boundaries of sight. They want to bridge the divide that separates them from the Divine. They believe that they can; and then some go on to believe that they are themselves that bridge. And while fanatics seek visions, Kant continues, governments are keen, for their own purposes, to provide them. They wish to keep their subjects compliant, and so they look for obstacles to impede any move towards self-reliance. Religion provides many such obstacles in the 'images and childish devices' it offers to those who wish to apprehend the Divine. These 'accessories' inhibit our spiritual development and make us the passive instruments of the Church. As with the Church, so with the State. Similar 'images and childish devices' make willing slaves of us all. The sublime, which refuses all images, is a weapon against these idolatries of religion and politics.

J.-F. Lyotard makes even more of this connection when answering the question 'What is Postmodernism?' Formlessness is what defines modern art (by which he means postmodern art). What is at stake in modern art is the making visible of the truth that there are some things which cannot be made visible, which do not have form. The artist's business is to invent allusions to the conceivable which cannot be presented. He thus becomes a witness to the unpresentable. The scriptural prohibition on presentation of the Absolute, together with Kant's gloss on it, Lyotard remarks, is pretty much all that needs to be said on the subject of the Sublime. Of course (he then adds), sublime paintings will 'present' something, but negatively. They will avoid figuration, and will be 'white' like one of Malevich's squares.

Thus in both Kant and Lyotard there is the implication that latent in the first prohibition is an aesthetic of great moment. The question is, however: is this a fruitful aesthetic for artists? More specifically, given that aniconic art, which in one version is an art of the Sublime, is mandated by the first prohibition: has this aesthetic provided the context for any Jewish art? Abstract Expressionism was for several reasons the most obvious candidate: it dealt in the Sublime, and some of its leading practitioners were Jews. Yet the Jewish Abstract Expressionists were largely indifferent to their origins and did not relate their art endeavours to any Jewish art tradition.

Part of the appeal of art to Rothko, suggests his biographer, was precisely that it was transgressive. Not only did it defy family expectations for a bourgeois career, it was also contrary to Jewish tradition. A Rothko admirer has perceptively noted the 'altar-like' character of his work, which offers the equivalent of an iconic symbol of a religious cult. Furthermore, the reluctance with which he gave up the figurative contains a hint of the non-Jewish nature of his art. Rothko himself wrote: 'Without monsters and gods, art cannot enact our drama: art's most profound moments express this frustration. When they were abandoned as untenable superstitions, art sank into melancholy.'

And what of Newman? By the titles to some of his works he certainly encouraged Jewish associations. Relying on these works, on an examination of some of the books on Jewish mysticism in Newman's library, and on a tendentious interpretation of the Abstract Expressionist programme, some critics have thereby claimed him for Jewish art. But they are, I think, quite mistaken. An artist's interest in Kabbalistic doctrines does not in itself make his art Jewish: consider the work of Anselm Kiefer (see p. 83). If there is any religious aspect to Newman's work, it is of a generalized sense of the numinous, which he as happily finds in pagan and Christian sources as in Jewish ones. 'We are reasserting,' he wrote, 'man's natural desire for the exalted.' Newman's non-figurative art no more cleaves to the prohibitions of the Second Commandment than does that of Malevich.

In themselves, those titles of his works that are drawn from the Hebrew Scriptures, or which allude to Jewish practices and belief, no

20 Mark Rothko,
Untitled, 1951

more affirm a Jewish identity than does his *Stations of the Cross* series in itself affirm a Christian one. There is more, however, to the Christianity of this series than the title. As viewers, we are required to recreate Jesus's own journey as we pass from picture to picture. The series invites an identification of spectator and subject which thus can only be repugnant to Jews. Lawrence Alloway says that Newman's 'concern with religious and mythical content never delivers an idol but a presence.' He is probably right; Newman does stay on the right side of this particular line. But it is a close thing, and is therefore very far indeed from any art which could properly be regarded as Jewish. What is more, Newman's theorizing of the sublime was itself unindebted to Jewish sources. His is not a Jewish art, not remotely.

What, then, is a Jewish art? One searches for examples of a Jewish aniconic art. Consider Alain Kirili's *Commandment II* (1980). It doesn't

21 Alain Kirili, *Commandment II*, 1980

22 Eli Content, *Untitled*, 1986–87

so much seek to represent the unrepresentable as represent the ban on representation (which is a lesser thing as a project). But notwithstanding its starkness, and a certain chthonic austerity, it fails as an art work, I think, because it has a random, arbitrary quality. Why those shapes, and not others? Why seventeen shapes, and not sixteen or eighteen? The work has no quality of inner necessity. It lacks aesthetic integrity.

Or consider Eli Content's *Untitled* (1986–87). For Avram Kampf, this is an artist who has expressly adopted the first prohibition as an aesthetic principle, filling his canvases, first, with heavily layered brushstrokes, and then adding Hebrew letters. But so far from thereby achieving effects of sublimity, all the artist manages is a certain idea of an illustrated manuscript, opaque and oppressive in its inverted ratio of text to picture.

Or, finally, consider Joshua Neustein's work, about which Kampf writes: '[this] imageless art ... is abstract because the God of Israel is an abstract concept.' For Neustein, Kampf continues, 'the Jewish God has replaced the icon ... it is not the belief in a personal God but the very purity of the abstract conception, its loftiness, its uncompromising

23 Joshua Neustein, *To Stella*, 1973–77

quality which excites the passion of the artist and guides him.' This is fine, but if one then considers a work such as *To Stella* (1973–77), it is impossible, I suggest, to derive from it such an aesthetic. There is the conception, and there is the work, but the vital connection between the two is missing. This is not a work that realizes the first prohibition.

None of these art works encourage optimism about a Jewish aniconic art. Perhaps it is precisely because the Sublime and more especially what might be termed the counter-Sublime are central to postmodernism that there isn't the space for a specifically Jewish art of the Sublime to emerge. Furthermore, the aniconic is a paradoxical art practice. The aniconic artist seeks to affirm the unrepresentable by his representations.

The Jewish aniconic artist declares: my subject will be the unrepresentability of God and the Jewish tradition's refusal of the iconic. And I will pursue it in the least promising of contexts, that of art. I will treat the first prohibition not as a ban on art works but as an invitation to make them. My works will set out to do what art works are supposed not to be able to do. I will take finite spaces and use them to convey infinity. I will appeal to my audience's vision when disclosing to them the invisibility of God. I will use images to communicate the imagelessness of the divine. I will, that is to say, seek to realize in art the prohibition of a certain kind of art. We are still waiting for this artist to appear.

Jewish iconicism

While there is a paucity of Jewish aniconic art, there is a surfeit of Jewish iconic works. There are far too many, and few of them have any value. Pictures of Rabbis, or of Jews at prayer, landscapes of Israel, figurines of scriptural characters: Jewish homes and public places are stuffed with such works. They are mostly timid, derivative items. It is as if their negotiation of the second prohibition, or their efforts to circumvent it (for example, by the invention of freakish creatures, or the depiction of incompletely limbed human beings), exhausted their makers' capacity for inventiveness or originality.

There are only two kinds of Jewish iconic art that are of interest. First, the kind that records communal life and practices when they are at risk (either because they are being given up, or because Jews themselves are in danger); this is an art of witness which includes Holocaust art. Second, the kind that appropriates Christian iconography for Jewish ends; this is an art of engagement. Jewish culture, to maintain itself, needs an art of witness. Jewish artists themselves need to practice an art of engagement (it is hard to be an artist if one shirks the encounter with Christian art).

These iconic arts of witness and engagement have a mixed record of success. Where Jewish art of the last hundred years is not illustrative of

Jewish life, it has tended to be merely imitative of Christian iconography. Either way, it copies: a milieu or a canon. The artist is unable to emancipate himself either from his Jewish subjects or his artist predecessors.

AN ART OF WITNESS

At a certain moment in Jewish history, it became common for Jewish artists who had (it was felt) moved outside of their communities to be summoned back in order to aid the work of national reconstruction. This, for example, was the burden of Ahad Ha-Am's response to the death of the Russian-Jewish artist, Mark Antokolsky (1843–1902).

Ahad Ha-am (lit. 'one of the people') was the name taken by Asher Ginsberg (1856–1927), a Zionist essayist and critic. Antokolsky was a Russian-Jewish academician celebrated in Russia for his work. For us, wrote Ha-Am in an article following the sculptor's death, there is a touch of bitterness in the homage which is paid him. Antokolsky worked for Russia, and Russia gets the glory now he is dead. But how much he might have given to his own people. How low we have sunk when men of genius go elsewhere to find scope for their creativity. The world would have benefited if he had stayed with his own people. How much greater would have been his contribution if he had portrayed Jewish life, of which he had a much more sympathetic understanding. He should have made a statue of Herod rather than Ivan the Terrible; he should have made a statue of the Gaon of Vilna rather than the medieval Russian monk Nestor. Ahad Ha-Am concludes: where are our Jewish artists?

This was a little unfair, both to Antokolsky himself and to numerous Jewish artists painting at the time. Many responded to his call, or to similar calls. There are now in existence any number of pictures of Jewish cityscapes, and of Jewish men in synagogues. Among American works, see for example Max Weber's *Adoration of the Moon* (1944) or Ben Shahn's *Sound in the Mulberry Trees* (1948). This is an art that is satisfied in merely putting a mirror up to Jewish life. Only when the mirror catches the gaze of a Rabbi does the artist risk creating an idol (for there is a tendency among certain kinds of Jews to treat Rabbinical portraits as amulets or talismans, or aids to holy living).

Holocaust art is at the edge of the modern Jewish art of witness. This is because it is an art which takes a subject that both defies and compels representation. It is rooted in a horror so specific as to deny altogether any element of the fantastic or the symbolic. The perplexing terrors of anti-Semitic persecution – for which Jewish artists were as unprepared as any other Jews – resist imaginative recastings, either as literature or art. The artist-witness can only document. He (or she) answers to the ethical imperative: remember! Karol Konieczny, a survivor of Buchenwald, wrote: 'an aesthete will not find material in [my drawings] for professional criticism. I wish them to be considered a living and shocking document of a world of horror and torment. I want the young to know how it was....' At a time when Jewish life was most

24 Max Weber, *Adoration of the Moon*, 1944
25 Ben Shahn, *Sound in the Mulberry Trees*, 1948

under threat, the desire both to record and to memorialize (in Holocaust art to record *is* to memorialize) was irresistible, of course. But it was also obligatory. This meant a necessarily figurative art, but one subordinate to the Jewish duty to bear witness. Holocaust art is thus a specially charged kind of art of witness.

AN ART OF ENGAGEMENT

To be a Jew is to take up an adversarial stance towards Christianity. For Jews, the doctrine of the Incarnation is, among other things, the gravest imaginable violation of the Second Commandment. An early medieval poem complained on behalf of Jews that they were forced 'to accept the despised idol as god, to bow to the image, to worship before it.' Christian art itself exacerbated bad relations between Jews and Christians, representing Jews as benighted, scary individuals, and Judaism as the defeated, blinded 'Synagoga'. In return, Jewish hostility towards Christianity has often taken the form of a repudiation of its central symbol, the crucified Christ. This remains the normative stance of Judaism. But it is plainly inadequate for the Jewish artist because to be an artist is to work within a tradition that continues to be indebted to Christianity. Following his election to the Royal Academy in 1840, Solomon Alexander Hart (1806–81) was introduced thus: 'This is Mr Hart whom we have just elected Academician ... Mr Hart is a Jew, and the Jews crucified our Saviour, but he is a very good man for all that, and we shall see something more of him now.' This has more than merely anecdotal weight. The crucifixion of which the Academician spoke with characteristic English insouciance remains at the very heart of the art canon. It was paradoxical, therefore, for a Jew to be elected to membership of the institutional custodian of that canon, the Royal Academy. Western culture continues to be one (as Jacques Aumant has argued) in which the paradigmatic image, indeed the very basis of any notion of the 'image', is the incarnation of God the Father in Jesus Christ. This is the culture with which the Jewish artist has, perforce, to engage.

Jewish artists have devised a number of ways of dealing with this problem. Most do so by either discounting their Jewishness or isolating themselves from the art tradition. These are the paths of rejection. Many of the finest Jewish artists of the 20th century took the first; too many inferior Jewish artists took the second. But neither, as a result, produced Jewish art of any real substance, the first because their art was not Jewish, the second because it tended to be at best minor and at worst kitsch.

This is, of course, somewhat simplistic. Qualifications and exceptions need to be made. There are very few Jewish artists of whom it is possible to say that there is no Jewish influence in their work. (Some would say that even the absence of any identifiable influence is evidence – of a repressed Jewishness. This has been proposed of Chaim Soutine.) There are a number of Jewish artists and craftsmen who have produced fine ornamental or decorative works within that Jewish art tradition that began with Bezalel. And there are many Jewish artists who experience the isolation from the art tradition as a burden rather than the willed consequence of any decision that they themselves have taken. Here is Gideon Ofrat, in his authoritative *One Hundred Years of Art in Israel* (New York, 1998), on Israeli art: 'It is an art grappling more with its deficiencies than utilizing its assets. It is deficient in classics, deficient in sublime European landscapes, deficient in cultural tradition, deficient in recognition (both Jewish and Israeli cultures grant literature the highest esteem).'

Other Jewish artists have taken paths of engagement. Some have sought to develop a Jewish iconography that is in some sense related to, while remaining independent of, Christian iconography. R.B. Kitaj is preeminent in this group, I believe. Other Jewish artists have appropriated Christian iconography for their own ends. For example Max Liebermann's *Jesus in the Temple* (1879) pointedly represents Jesus as a Jew (Jews have sometimes re-adopted Jesus as a provocation to anti-Semites). And, rather more inventively, David Bomberg's *Hear O Israel*

26 Max Liebermann, *Jesus in the Temple*, 1879

(1955) adapts El Greco's *Christ Carrying the Cross* (1590–95). Still others have sought, by acts of individual artistic will, to assert an equivalence in authority of Jewish and Christian iconographic traditions. This is somewhat quixotic: see Brussilovsky's *Two Ideas* (1984).

Chagall is exceptional in that his work combines these paths. He was not always able, of course, to pull off this combination of innovative Jewish and adapted Christian iconography. His crucifixion paintings, in particular, are an unhappy amalgam of iconographies, and lack coherence. They also follow a certain course. Jewish art in the first centuries CE is replete with pagan themes and techniques. At the Dura synagogue, for example, above the shrine for the Torah there is a picture of Orpheus enchanting the animals. And Moses is portrayed in superhuman dimensions, a typical device in pagan art when representing gods or heroes. Rosenzweig was quite wrong when he insisted that the forms of inner Jewish life are quite distinct from all apparent parallels in civilizations, and specifically that the art of the synagogue has no living

27 David Bomberg, *Hear O Israel*, 1955
28 El Greco, *Christ Carrying the Cross*, 1590–95

29 Anatolii Brussilovsky, *Two Ideas*, 1984

relation with other art. Quite to the contrary, in fact. Jewish art has invariably borrowed from the dominant, non-Jewish artistic repertoire. What Chagall's career demonstrates is that the Jewish artist can also contribute to that repertoire. (And continue to contribute: having invented a style, Chagall contented himself with reproducing it, to the point of self-parody.) But for a Jewish art, this in itself is not enough.

I suspect that he knew this himself. This, at any rate, is how I interpret the triptych *Resistance* (1937–48), *Resurrection* (1937–48), and *Liberation* (1937–52). While the first two paintings are crucifixion scenes, in the third the Jew takes flight with his violin, amid the festivities that crowd the canvas. The painting positively bustles. It contains a wedding complete with canopy and musicians, political rallies and red flags, parents and small children, and an artist and his easel. And the cross? You can just see it, at the top left-hand corner of the picture, next to the figure of Moses. This is the mere trace of a crucifixion, bleached and scratchy.

Both Jewish lawgiver and Christian messiah are thus on the border of the work. But while the one is a peripheral yet minatory presence, the other is an absence. A diminished Moses rages at Israelite idolatry;

30 Marc Chagall, *Resistance*, 1937–48
31 Marc Chagall, *Resurrection*, 1937–48
32 Marc Chagall, *Liberation*, 1937–52

the white lines of the crucifixion are as erasure marks made on a page. Together they define Chagall's problematic: a certain awareness of the prohibition against images combined with a susceptibility to Christian iconography.

Liberation may be regarded as a celebration not just of Jewish survival of Nazi terror, but of the emergence of a Jewish iconography free of Christian derivation and yet also strong enough to push the Mosaic interdictions to the margin. It was originally entitled *Hatikva* ('the Hope'), which is the name of the Israeli national anthem. National and artistic independence were to be related, each one to the other, but then Chagall changed his mind (he might have thought that the title conferred on the collective project of nation-building some tacit authority to direct the singular projects of individual artists). The triptych remains, however, a kind of visual parable for the Jewish artist. It is full of hope, and it points the way.

Komar and Melamid: a Jewish iconoclasm

There is a gap between what Jewish art can be (that is, what the Second Commandment mandates) and what it actually is. The Jewish aesthetic contains a promise which has yet fully to be realized by Jewish artists. There is little aniconic art; there is too much inferior iconic art; what, then, of iconoclastic art?

Given the propensity of the art work to idolatrous usages, and the proximity of the image to the icon, and of the icon to the idol, there is a paradoxical, even self-cancelling quality about iconoclastic art. Its object is to destroy the idol, even at the risk of undoing itself. It exists in order to contribute to the battle against idolatry, and hazards its own extinction in the process. It is therefore, unavoidably, an art of irony. It views itself with some scepticism.

Jews have an obligation to extirpate idolatry, and to destroy idols. The 19th-century sage R. Samson Raphael Hirsch could not have been clearer: 'You must wherever and whenever you can, destroy all visible signs of idolatry. He who obtains possession of an idol ... must destroy it, pulverize it and scatter it into wind or water.' Notwithstanding this, Jewish iconoclasm has tended to be pacific (perhaps in part for want of opportunities). It has not typically been pursued by pamphleteers or by crowds armed with clubs. While the common view is that Abraham broke his father Terah's idols, Maimonides prefers to praise the patriarch as the first person who opposed idolatry 'by arguments and by soft and persuasive speech'.

To engage the idol in a war of annihilation is to pay to it an unwarranted compliment. Turn it on its head, decorate it with graffiti, give it a funny moustache – these are gestures of disrespect which rob the idol of its aura. They leave the idol itself standing, but more effectively diminished. The *Kitzur Shulchan Aruch*, restating a Talmudic exception, stipulates that 'all kinds of mockery are forbidden, except mockery of idols which is permitted.' Indeed, it is enjoined. Maryan S. Maryan's *Personage with Donkey Ears* (1962) is a good example of just this kind of sanctioned

33 Maryan S. Maryan, *Personage with Donkey Ears*, 1962

34 Ferdinand Staeger, *SS on Guard*, n.d.
35 Rudolf Otto, *Ready for Battle*, n.d.

mockery. Compare it with Ferdinand Staeger's pseudo-religious *SS on Guard* (n.d.) and Rudolf Otto's bombastic *Ready for Battle* (n.d.). The Nazi is revealed by Maryan in all his ugly stupidity. The point about this kind of iconoclasm is not so much that it mocks or breaks idols as that it tells the truth about them; or rather, it tells the truth about them *by* breaking them or mocking them.

Mockery need not be a feeble alternative to physical destruction, to be pursued by a Diaspora Jewry without the means to harm in any other way (the Jewish form of defensive combat, as N. Sokolow put it). It is a subtler, more effective means of idol-breaking. It combines iconoclastic and creative impulses. And it is ambitious. It doesn't seek to destroy this or that idol, but the system of idolatry. Break one idol, and others remain (whatever the loss of collective esteem or prestige that they may suffer by the easy damage to one of their number). But subvert the very form of the representation and nothing is left.

The Jewish sculptor Naum Aronson refused to make statues of French military leaders in the aftermath of World War I. In an act of disciplined abstention from the 'statuemania' of the times, he would not carve secular idols. Between the abstentionism of an Aronson and the exterminationism of an idol-breaker lies the work of Komar and Melamid. They preserve the idol while subjecting it to a critique; indeed, they revive the idol they ironize. In a reverse movement to the typical iconoclast, the artists restore the hated idol.

Their art has two iconoclastic aspects, the aesthetic and the political. That is to say, it is sceptical of claims made both by art itself and on its behalf, claims that are in turn made both in the interests of aestheticism and totalitarianism. This iconoclasm has as its target the conviction that either Art or the State will redeem us.

In 1973 the two artists published a spoof monograph, *A. Ziablov*. This purported to tell the story of an 18th-century serf who broke with the prevailing art practices of his time by painting abstract pictures. Rejected by the Academy, and forced to copy the work of other, less daring artists, he killed himself. Up to this point, it is a story that conforms to a prevailing, modern type: the misunderstood artist, ahead of his time, spurned by an aggressively ignorant establishment. That Apelles Ziablov is a serf gives the story a political thrust too. As serf and avant-gardiste, he is doubly disadvantaged, doubly progressive.

Yet this serf paints his pictures to decorate the torture chambers of his master, the landowner Striuskii. Ziablov, representative of the avant-garde, is thereby inculpated in the cruellest expressions of political reaction. He is Striuskii's accomplice. He may be the victim of a repressive society, but he is also its accessory. And there is more. Striuskii himself remonstrates with Ziablov: your iconoclasm is incomplete. Your purely abstract art is not as iconoclastic as the 'stark style [of] the Jews of yesteryear and today' (an obscure but telling phrase). Why do you not adopt their style? And: your struggle against the idolatry of figurative art is too selective. Why do you not contest the other idols of the day? Ziablov has no answer to either question. His iconoclasm misses its mark. The two projects of Komar and Melamid I want to consider now, *Monumental Propaganda* and *Painting by Numbers*, do not.

POLITICAL ICONOCLASM

Russian art has its origins in the iconic tradition of Byzantium; Socialist Realism returned to that tradition for its own political purposes; contemporary Russian art reprises the iconic, articulating it in new registers.

There is, for example, Mikhail Shvartsman's *Space of the Trinity* (1986), with its celebration of the Christian mystery. This artist refers to his pictures as 'hieratures'; he says that an angel guides his hand when he paints. There is Simen Faibisovich's refusal of the iconic: the bathers in *Before Bathing* (1988) are just bathers. And there is the contrasting overstatement of the iconic, as in Aleksei Sundokov's *Prolonged and Undiminished Applause* (1987), with its bleached-out faces, indistinct against the precisely defined features of the icon-leaders of the USSR.

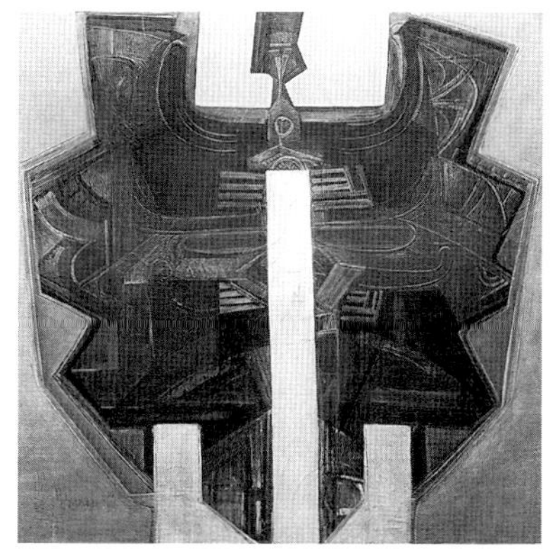

36 Mikhail Shvartsman, *Space of the Trinity*, 1986

37 Aleksei Sundokov, *Prolonged and Undiminished Applause*, 1987
38 Simen Faibisovich, *Before Bathing*, 1988

39 Mikhail Grobman, *Our Power is in Zionism*, 1996

It is in the ironizing of the iconic that I find a distinctly Jewish engagement (though never, of course, an exclusively Jewish engagement). In addition to Komar and Melamid, this is an aspect of the work of a number of other Russian-Jewish artists. There is, for instance, Mikhail Grobman, whose 1996 work *Our Power is in Zionism* reduces to a nonsense the anti-Semitic sloganizing of the Soviet State. But it is Komar and Melamid who develop this iconoclasm furthest. In their hands it ceases to be the means for occasional protest and becomes instead an aesthetic.

In the wake of de-Stalinization, many sculptures, frescoes and paintings were smashed or burned. Portraits – especially group portraits – were altered in familiar ways, with discredited figures being painted out. Then, with the collapse of Communism, the same process repeated itself, but this time as a series of local initiatives. They were protests against the State, and not undertakings by the State to rewrite its own history. But there was a parallel between the earlier State-sponsored iconoclasm and the more recent popular iconoclasm: the desire to erase the past.

In response to this work of destruction, Komar and Melamid published an appeal to artists and to the then Russian president, Boris Yeltsin, in the art journal *Artforum*. It appeared in May 1992, and was entitled: 'What is to Be Done with Monumental Propaganda?' The title itself contained a clue to the answer they proposed. 'What is to Be Done?' was the title of a celebrated work by Lenin, who in turn took it from what at one time was an even more celebrated work by Chernyshevski. Komar and Melamid were using the same formula, but against the established use. They adopted it, and turned it against itself – exactly what they proposed doing with the monumental propaganda, and indeed very like the way that spies were 'turned' during the Cold War. They worked for one side; then they worked for the other side.

'Today,' the artists began, 'any effort to save Russia's Socialist Realist monuments from destruction would surely be seen as an attempt to preserve a totalitarian tradition.' But, they continued, this need not be so. 'We propose neither worship nor annihilation of these monuments, but a creative collaboration with them.' This collaboration is of an ironic nature, of course. They do not wish merely to continue the life of these monuments, but to transform them. The monuments comprise opportunities for art. And therefore also for a certain kind of moral reckoning. Why not, they suggest, 'lift a statue by hydraulic cranes, as if to remove it, but then leave it hanging in the air, ambiguously arresting the moment of dismantlement and extending it into eternal retribution?'

What about adding, they inquire, the letters 'ISM' to the leader's name at Lenin's mausoleum, to make it the 'symbolic grave of Leninist theory and practice?' As for the statue of the founder of the Soviet secret police, Felix Dzerzhinsky: don't remove it from opposite KGB headquarters, instead supplement it with bronze figures of the people who climbed on it in August 1991 to put a noose around its neck. The possibilities are almost infinite, and unprecedented. Why don't we plant a

40 Komar and Melamid, statue of Felix Dzerzhinsky (detail), from 'Monumental Propaganda', 1993
41 Komar and Melamid, statue of Karl Marx (detail), from 'Monumental Propaganda', 1993
42 Vera Mukhina, *Worker and Peasant*, 1937
43 Art Spiegelman, *One Step Forward, Two Steps Back (After)*, 1992

huge pigeon on the head of one of the 'de-throned statues' of Lenin? Why not up-end the monument to Marx in front of the Bolshoi Theatre? These are iconoclastic gestures purified of the violence that usually accompanies such acts. They demote the symbols of totalitarian power, subordinating them to the free, playful imagination of the artist.

'We can turn Moscow,' propose Komar and Melamid, 'into a phantasmagoric garden of post-totalitarian art.' They want to make something new out of the given, to transform something inert into art. In their open letter to Yeltsin, they asked: 'How long will people continue worshipping or destroying things, never knowing other alternatives?' A number of artists responded. One of my favourites is Art Spiegelman's proposal to have the man and woman representing *The Proletariat and Agriculture* striding off their pedestal into a void.

While they would do this (partly, at least) as an act of remembrance, they understate the iconoclasm of the project when they draw a parallel with the Renaissance use of Classical mythology: 'The fall of communism was like the fall of the Roman Empire.... In the Renaissance, the old Latin heroes, the mythic giants, were revived, woke up once more and put to use.... The fallen idols had new roles in Renaissance art, a new life. That is what we are trying to do in the post-totalitarian, post-socialist realist art: give new life to the old gods.' But part of *their* project, one rejoins – and what distinguishes it, say, from Raphael's – is to prevent the old god Stalin from returning. One means of ensuring that this never will happen is to keep alive the memory of his deeds in a way that denies them their potency.

Destroying the idol just leaves an empty space, one which another idol may occupy. But preserving the idol, while denying it its bogus magic, strikes a telling blow against all false gods. To defeat your adversary and bury him is one thing. To dress him in a jester's costume and have him perform for you is another, more crushing, victory. He survives to give witness to his own powerlessness. One need not fear his return because he already has returned, in a guise which poses no threat at all.

ART ICONOCLASM

There is, however fortuitously, a convergence of Jewish aesthetics and the anti-representational course taken by modern art. But there is a much greater divergence between Jewish aesthetics and certain more general philosophical perspectives on art. The gap narrowed between what Judaism has to say about art and the art works that were actually being made; but the gap between art's status in Judaism and its status in the wider world grew bigger.

From about the end of the 18th century, and in contrast with the view of art as decorative or ornamental (the conventional Jewish view – the idea of a Jewish iconoclastic art is mine), a number of increasingly extravagant claims for art came to be made. This was, for example, the principal thrust of much German philosophy from Kant onwards. The privileged place given there to art – that is to say, to 'Art' rather than this or that particular art work – could not be in more radical contrast to the modesty of art's standing in the Jewish world.

In very general terms, I would put it like this. By the time art had begun to explore the possibilities of the abstract, art theory had developed an understanding of the art work, and of aesthetic appreciation, which was in its essential nature idolatrous. Art became its own end, autotelic – not an accompaniment to something else, but the thing itself. It was promoted as a substitute for religion, and art appreciation became analogous to, and then a substitute for, religious experience. Until about the middle of the 19th century, the art work was only at risk of being worshipped or destroyed for what it represented. Since then, however, it has faced the new risks of being worshipped or destroyed for what it itself is.

This is, of course, a complex, fractured story to tell, and I can only tell it here in overstated and schematic language. It has a number of aspects. There is the notion of the artist as a creator – if not a rival to God, at least equal to Him in his own field. There is the notion of the art work itself as being a gift from the artist to mankind – Son, so to speak, to the artist Father. And there is the notion of the experience of the art work as being in some sense redemptive. While in its formulation, this account is plainly indebted to Christianity, in its historical emergence it is the consequence of a crisis in Christian faith. It preserves the forms of faith while giving them new content. It is deeply indebted to German Idealist philosophy; it is deeply inimical to the Jewish tradition. Rosenzweig, writing very carefully, argued that Idealism 'apotheosized art'. Idealists worshipped something that was in truth but 'a single limb torn loose from the whole body of humanity'.

This account exists in a number of versions; certainly, it has never (so far as I am aware) been expressed as baldly as I have just done. It is perhaps best regarded as the silent premise of the modern understanding of art, a premise which explains, for example, why the destruction of art works is often experienced, and then described, as sacrilege or desecration.

I can do no more here than to point to representative moments in its articulation. There is, for example, Kant's *Critique of Judgment*, which confers on aesthetic judgment a privileged status; there is the modernist art work's self-understanding – what I will call its immanent aesthetic – which expects from its audience a certain kind of reverence; there is the 'aesthetic alibi', advanced by the artist in support of a claim for exemption from legal regulation or moral censure; and there is modern connoisseurship, the rituals and practices of which are like nothing so much as those of the religious votary. This is something of a miscellany, but taken together it suggests (I can argue no more strongly than this) an ideology of art which can fairly be described as idolatrous.

Throughout, one finds a confusion of art and religion, a certain bogus sanctification of art, which one can deplore either in the name of religion itself or in the name of a disenchanted secularism. It is inconsistent, certainly, with any specifically Jewish understanding of the limits of art and the subaltern nature of the artist. 'It is no coincidence,' said Rosenzweig, 'that many great artists have sooner or later taken leave of the falsehood of artistic life, and cast their magic wand with Prospero into the sea in order to live out their lives humanly, as simple mortals.' The Jewish artist Mordechai Ardon puts the tension between the Jewish imperative and the art imperative like this:

> No getting away from it! Queer Jerusalem always has some orders to give! 'Thou shalt...' 'Thou shalt not...' – like a black woodpecker Jerusalem always knocks at your bark: thou ... thou ... thou [...] As if life could be lived in the 'thou' and as if being alive could only manifest itself in conjunction with the 'thou'.... That's the problem: the 'you' does not play any part in modern art. Artists are suns revolving on their own axes.

For the Jew, this elevation of art and artists is to be deplored. The formula 'art for art's sake' is false in that it recognizes no master for art, and immoral in that it liberates the artist from his duties as a man. Art in general substitutes for objects mere images. These images do not make the objects intelligible; only concepts can do that. Art is at best decorative. The image is a mere shadow of being; art lets go of its prey for the shadow. It is disengaged; in a world of initiative and responsibility, it constitutes a dimension of evasion. The image is an idol. Images bewitch the most lucid writer; as for the artist, he practises idolatry. Every art work is in the end a statue; every statue denies time, that is, the historicity of our world. This denial of historicity, which is an embracing of fate, is pagan. Art is pagan, and it is also Christianity's concession to paganism, a concession that Judaism itself is not required to make. Great art is non-Jewish art, accessible to Jews thanks to the fact that they live among Christians. I paraphrase the Jewish philosopher Emmanuel Levinas, in whose work one may find the most compelling restatement of the Jewish deprecation of art. The only serious rival to Levinas in this respect is Theodor Adorno.

The Jewish artist is responsive to this cultural reflex of deprecation. His work, when it does not take refuge in the decorative (which meekly protests: I am harmless, do not ban me), displays a creative scepticism not just towards art's subjects but also towards its purposes. By creative scepticism I mean something like an art-making iconoclasm, that is, an art which turns against Art. The Jewish artist contests the illegitimate uses to which art has been put, either instrumentalized or idolized, either treated as a mere means or as the ultimate end. But it is always, whether the one or the other, accorded a false authority. Art tends to present images as unchallengeable 'givens'. Pictures are anti-discursive, which makes them difficult to contest. The art iconoclast turns this difficulty into a vocation.

Komar and Melamid presented their 'Painting by Numbers' project as a 'scientific guide to art'. For just over a week in 1993, a telephone survey of Americans was conducted. There were also town-hall meetings. The expressed object was to discover what Americans want in their art. Komar and Melamid then painted two pictures derived from the responses, one of which was a composite of everything that the respondents most wanted, the other of what they least wanted. They called the pictures *America's Most Wanted* and *America's Most Unwanted*. They then conducted similar surveys in a number of other countries. What most surprised them, they said later, was the 'sameness' of majority opinion. What had been coerced under Communism arose spontaneously in democracy. The blue landscape unites the world. 'Can you believe it?' they exclaim, 'Kenya and Iceland!' 'And they both want blue landscapes.'

44 Komar and Melamid, *America's Most Wanted*, 1994
45 Komar and Melamid, *America's Most Unwanted*, 1994

46 Komar and Melamid, *Kenya's Most Wanted*, 1996
47 Komar and Melamid, *Kenya's Most Unwanted*, 1996

48 Komar and Melamid, *Iceland's Most Unwanted*, 1995
49 Komar and Melamid, *Iceland's Most Wanted*, 1995

50 From *The Pennysaver*, Ithaca, New York, 19–26 October 1994

In an interview that they gave about the project, they explained that they wanted people to be 'horrified' by the *Most Wanted* pictures, so that gradually public taste would change. This pedagogic, gently mocking stance teases while it instructs. Komar and Melamid are ironic Bezalels – producing art works for the adornment of consumers' homes. See, for example, the poster 'What do YOU want...'. They choose their masters, 'the people'. But it is not enough to say that the 'joke' is on 'the people' (as one critic has suggested), because the joke is on everyone and everything else too. Nothing and no one escapes. The irony corrodes the esteem in which each and every element in the art world is held. These artists have made, as Melamid says, 'a totally dissident art'.

It is, Komar adds, a notion of 'art as entertainment that poses questions'. It is not self-important; among the questions it poses are a number directed at the institution of art itself. The interrogation is in part a self-interrogation. Their artistic undertaking is thus at once both modest and challenging. They do not make exaggerated claims for their art, or for art in general. 'We have lost,' they say, 'our belief that we are the minority which *knows*.' They made a series of 'Post Art' works by painting facsimiles of iconic modern images (by Warhol, Lichtenstein and Indiana) and then blow-torching them. They are avant-gardiste in their principled refusal of the myths of the avant-garde. And they will find collaborators in the unlikeliest of places: 'Recently we collaborated with an elephant, who by the way, is an abstract painter; and before that we worked with a realist dog.'

Art-making dogs and elephants, however gifted, have little in common with even the most modest conception of the artist. They have nothing at all in common with the very exalted conception that was a commonplace among members of the art movement from which Komar and Melamid themselves emerged. Mikhail Grobman's vatic pronouncement, 'he who thinks or prophesies is an artist', is typical of its time and place. Many other 'Second Culture' artists, the critic Yevgeni Barabanov has explained, thought likewise. To them the artist

51 Komar and Melamid, *Post Art No. 1 (Warhol)*, 1973

was a Creator, a Demigod, a mediator between different worlds – cosmos and chaos, nature and culture, spirit and flesh. Komar and Melamid are not impressed with any of this. They regard it – I believe correctly – as so much pseudo-theology: 'The old romantic maxim that it is not genius [which] must understand the people but rather people who must understand the genius brings to mind the notion of God's inscrutability.' The cult of art as the supreme value is absurd, they continue, the reflex of a religious faith that has lost its true object: 'belief in art, faith in art, starts with atheism.' Artists and critics 'worship art as something sacred, a separate church. Atheism believes in art adamantly; I know from Russia. It's a last refuge of spirituality, because in Russia artists are the most sacred of the sacred people.'

The nature of this 'totally dissident art', in which everyone is mocked, is nicely illustrated by a joke Melamid tells in the *Painting by Numbers* interview. They executed, he says, a huge commission for the lobby of the tallest building in Los Angeles. When they were tendering for the commission, they repeated to the owner of the building ('[he] owns a lot of skyscrapers – he's a very, very rich man') a joke that they had once told in Jersey City. They were there to make pictures for a small Catholic church: 'Listen, we are not Michelangelo, but Jersey City is not Rome.' Melamid continues:

> I repeated this joke to this guy and he liked it. So at the opening of this wall in L.A., a huge event, he said, Oh, these funny Russian guys, they said a really funny thing, and he repeated this, and of course the audience laughed. So in answer to him, I said: 'We're not Michelangelo, that's for sure, and L.A. [is] not Rome, but you're not Medici.

Though I have separated out the two Komar and Melamid projects – 'Monumental Propaganda' and 'Painting by Numbers' – there is a relation between political idolatry and art idolatry. Heidegger, writing from a National Socialist perspective, put it thus: 'the art work should be a celebration of the *Volksgemeinschaft*: it should be *the* religion.' And this is Rosenzweig, from an antithetical perspective: 'Those eternal gods of paganism, in which [pagan society] survives until the end of time, the state and art, the former the idol of materialists, the latter the idol of the personalists.' Lenin once said that he disapproved of 'iconoclasts in painting'. He had in mind the point at which art iconoclasm and political iconoclasm cross, that is, the place where Komar and Melamid practice their art.

Iconoclasms

A certain diffuse, rather diluted iconoclasm is characteristic of much art thinking of the last hundred and fifty years. When the art critic Louis Edmond Duranty remarked in 1856 that 'if I had had some matches I would have set fire to [the Louvre], with the intimate conviction that I was serving the art of the future' he was only expressing in provocative form what had already become a cultural cliché: that the existing is an obstacle to the emergence of the new, and thus has to be cleared away. As another critic put it, just under fifty years later: 'to imagine a new art, one must break the old art. And so the new art appears as a kind of iconoclasticism [*sic*].' There is nothing very interesting about this kind of 'iconoclasm' and it barely deserves the name.

But there are in addition three distinct engagements with the iconoclastic in modern art that are worth noting, not least because they are so different from the Jewish iconoclasm that I find instantiated in Komar and Melamid. I refer to the anti-art of Marcel Duchamp, the auto-destructive art of Gustav Metzger, and the art of Anselm Kiefer.

Neither art nor non-art, many of Duchamp's interventions in the art world made questionable the assumptions on which that world was, and continues to be, based: the necessary originality of the artist, and the necessary uniqueness and beauty of the art object. Having extricated himself from all existing schools of art by 1911, he spent a decade or

52 Marcel Duchamp, *L.H.O.O.Q.*, 1919
53 Alfred Stieglitz, Marcel Duchamp's *Fountain*, 1917

more devising provocations, works intended to stand outside art. He described *L.H.O.O.Q.* (1919) as 'a combination readymade and iconoclastic Dadaism'. Duchamp's ambition was to abolish the distinction between the aesthetic and the non-aesthetic, between art and non-art. That his work was nonetheless appropriated to art was thus a matter of regret for him: 'When I discovered readymades I thought to discourage aesthetics. I threw the bottle-rack and urinal in their faces and now they admire them for their aesthetic beauty.'

These artistic provocations have an antagonistic relation to art; to adopt the Dadaist term, they are 'anti-art'. Anti-art is hostile not just to art itself but also to art's audiences. Sometimes expressing hostility to art's typical audience exhausts the object of the work. The best kind of provocation, however, when addressed to the best kind of audience, provokes thought rather than mere reflexes of outrage. But just as they are not art, so they are not in themselves philosophy. They cannot be, because they remain concrete, physical, particular.

Duchamp's work is to be distinguished from Jewish iconoclasm in two respects: by the exalted status it claims by implication for the artist, and by the nature of its ingenious and provocative adaptation of Christian iconography. As to the first: the 'readymade', Duchamp said, was an 'everyday commodity promoted to the dignity of a work of art by the mere choice of the artist.' The Duchampian artist claims the power to transform the base metal of everyday into the gold of art. The urinal ceases to be an object of utility and becomes one of contemplation, no longer a mere undifferentiable instance of the mass-produced but a unique work. The Duchampian artist is quite unlike, then, one kind of Jewish artist, the Bezalelian artist, modestly crafting artifacts for the greater glory of his religion. And as to the second: Alfred Stieglitz photographed *Fountain* with a shadow falling across it. The effect is to suggest a veil, and the piece was renamed 'Madonna of the Bathroom'. To seek to evoke the Virgin and Child by the presentation of a urinal is blasphemous, not iconoclastic; the same applies to *Large Glass*, with its likeness to the Assumption of the Virgin (Duchamp described the work as a 'sort of apotheosis of Virginity'). The blasphemer affirms the idol's power even as he abuses it. The iconoclast abuses the idol to demonstrate its lack of power. Duchamp is a blasphemer, Komar and Melamid are iconoclasts.

Gustav Metzger takes a material aspect of all art works, that is, their unavoidable impermanence, and makes this the principal feature of his aesthetic. He turns a limitation into an opportunity. Metzger paints with acid on nylon screens, and uses metals that rust. His installations are short-lived; he celebrates the transitory. One planned event was stopped

54 Gustav Metzger, *South Bank Demonstration*, 3 July 1961

on grounds of public safety. His 'works' are intended to elude the embrace of the art economy; they cannot be bought. He once tried to organize an art strike ('the most extreme collective challenge that artists can make to the State'). Though he was born of Polish-Jewish parents, Metzger's art is not a Jewish art.

Metzger's manifesto, 'Auto-destructive art' (1965), seeks to justify an art which cannot exist for long enough to justify itself. (Another advocate of the auto-destructive, Franz Kline, conceded that the theory was more advanced than the practice.) Auto-destructive art, Metzger insists, is not the therapeutic instrument of a frustrated iconoclast. The theme of destruction is common to several major modern art movements: Cubism, Futurism, Dadaism. As Mondrian states, the importance of destruction in art is understated. Auto-destructive art speaks of the pleasure and liberation in destruction. Its ambitions are not modest. It aims to save society. It wants to change people. It undermines beliefs, prejudices, fears. It sets up a mirror to reality: society is deteriorating, so should sculpture. Auto-destructive art re-enacts society's obsession with destruction. The artist does not want to give his work to a society as foul as this one. So auto-destructive art becomes a kind of boycott of art galleries, which are mere capitalist institutions, boxes of deceit.

Metzger is not an iconoclast. He wants to save art from the art industry just as he wants to save art audiences from capitalism. He reveres art, and reveres art-making. For him, the artist is a seer, and his manifestos are prophetic indictments. This is not a Jewish aesthetic. It posits an art which is redemptive, neither useful nor decorative. It is not an art alive to art's limitations.

Anselm Kiefer's work represents the most important contemporary engagement of art with the iconoclastic. What he has to say about certain of his projects is reminiscent of Komar and Melamid's programme. Here, for example, is Kiefer on Albert Speer's buildings: 'I was fascinated by these buildings, and I wanted to transform them. You know, normally you don't destroy buildings. You do it sometimes, but usually you transform them, like the Christians transformed old temples of the Pantheon into Christian churches.... I transformed these old buildings and gave them a new destiny, a new meaning. Because you never succeed in really destroying something, it always lives, and it's more efficient to *transform* than to destroy. Because the thing that is destroyed survives more than the thing that's transformed.'

And yet Kiefer is not an iconoclast but rather an artist who plays with iconoclasm in order to reaffirm a pagan aesthetic. The modern objects of iconoclasm – the deification of Art and State – become occasions for his art. He plays with them, as themes. The theme of the religion of art becomes the occasion for *Saint Eustace* (1974): the stag with the palette is a revision of Dürer's stag with a crucifix in his *Saint Eustace* (*c.* 1500–1). The theme of art's complicity with political power becomes the occasion for *Herzeleide* (1979): the mother with the palette is a revision of a Nazi-period photograph which shows a mother gazing at a document containing Third Reich legislation.

We must not confuse the post-Christian with the Jewish. It is much more likely to be the *pre*-Jewish. Kiefer's work is not a return to Jewish prohibitions. It is not a Jewish art, it is a pagan art. And this of course means, as one student of his work has expressed it, that his work takes up Jewish subjects with a determined if not troubling persistence. Consider, for example, Kiefer's praise for Aaron, whom he has painted: 'the handsome politician and intermediary, who gave room to the people with the golden calf.' Kiefer has suggested that 'there is no one god for all. Each man has his own....' And so he has painted a picture entitled *Every Man Stands Beneath His Own Dome of Heaven* (1970) which makes just this point. Iconoclasm itself becomes an occasion for his art: see *Iconoclastic Controversy* (1980). Kiefer represents the iconoclasts as an army, tanks taking aim at a palette. He returns in his work repeatedly to the theme of the artist as victim, elevated but at risk, Duchampian in his authority but vulnerable to attack. Kiefer's iconoclasm – if it is that at all, and not a pagan impatience with monotheism – is directed against

55 Anselm Kiefer, *Saint Eustace*, 1974
56 Albrecht Dürer, *Saint Eustace* (detail), *c.* 1500–1
57 Anselm Kiefer, *Herzeleide*, 1979

58 Anselm Kiefer, *Every Man Stands Beneath His Own Dome of Heaven*, 1970
59 Anselm Kiefer, *Iconoclastic Controversy*, 1980

the Absolute, not against idols. He is with Aaron and against Bezalel. But more than that, he is with Terah and against Abraham. Indeed, his art is Terah's revenge.

And against the self-importance of all three artists, Komar and Melamid's irony is directed at themselves as much as at Art and its institutions, and the State and *its* institutions. There are, of course, different kinds of irony. There is irony as a mode of address, which consists of saying either the opposite of what one means or something different from what one means. This is a rhetorical technique, a means by which one may expose one's interlocutor's folly. It is a species of disrespect, and is akin to mockery. Then there is irony as a mode of thought, which consists of regarding both one's own beliefs and the beliefs of others with comparable (if not quite the same) scepticism. This is to be an ironist. The ironist holds his beliefs to be both contingent and fragile, and holds no one else's beliefs to be any better secured. He also does not believe it is possible to adjudicate between sets of beliefs. One may speak ironically; one may be an ironist. The two are distinct. The one is a stratagem to adopt, or not; the other is a cast of mind. While a dogmatist may thus on occasion be ironic, he can never be an ironist.

Komar and Melamid are, in their artistic practice, ironists. This is not a characteristic of Judaism. Rather, then, than regarding their work as Jewish, might it not be simpler merely to say of it that it has a relation with the Second Commandment? Perhaps even that it is work which a Jewish aesthetics derived from the prohibitions is singularly well-equipped to understand? This is so, but I think that one can go a little further. Fackenheim cites a midrash: 'Who is a Jew? One who testifies against idols.' Grant the adequacy of the definition and Komar and Melamid become exemplary Jews, their work an exemplary Jewish art.

SOME ANXIETIES ABOUT ICONOCLASM

Iconoclasm has a place in two quite distinct histories: the history of the making of art works, and the history of their loss. It is indeed what connects two histories that in other respects are mutually exclusive. The iconoclast can be an artist or an enemy of art, and sometimes he can be both. And though the iconoclasm I praise in this book is within the first history – it leads not to the loss of existing works but the creation of new ones, or substitutes of a kind that in some manner preserve the original work – it would be wrong to overlook a certain continuity that iconoclasm of any type has with the intentional destruction of art, and beyond that, the persecution of artists. One has to be careful.

Iconoclasm is regarded too uncritically these days; just about anybody can earn the name. (*The Jerusalem Report* – of all journals! – described Holocaust-denier David Irving as an 'iconoclast, consciously challenging the consensus on the greatest crime of the 20th century'.) Desecrators of Jewish cemeteries are desperate iconoclasts. As the depraved heirs to a Christian iconicism, they think the gravestones that they violate are Jewish icons. Whenever people get too enthusiastic about iconoclasm they should think of the Nazi destruction of art, and the 'Degenerate Art' exhibition of 1937. The young Nazis pictured here are iconoclasts: note their glee as they go about their work of incineration. They were not alone. In 1933 some German artists published a manifesto calling for 'cosmopolitan or Bolshevist' art works to be

60 Members of Hitler Youth burning books, Berlin 1933

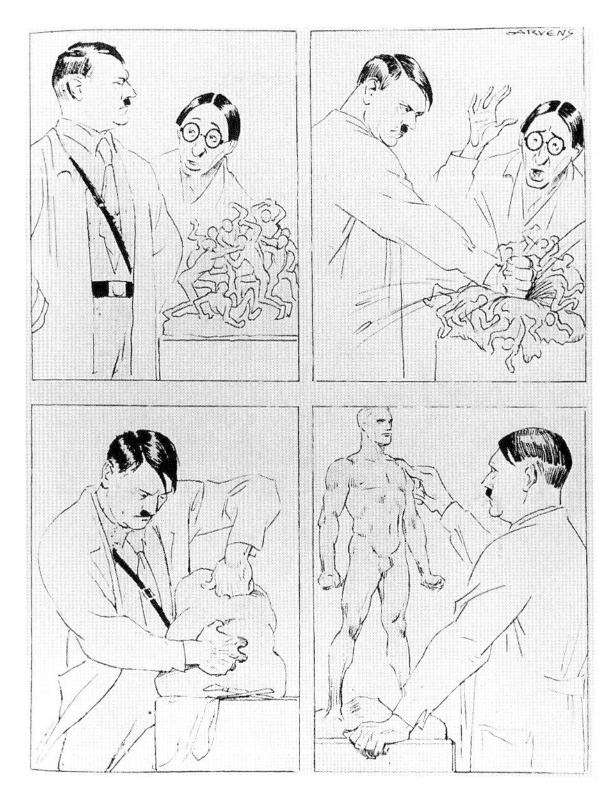

61 Garvens, 'The Sculptor of Germany', published in *Jugend*, 1933

destroyed: 'these works of anti-art ... can serve as fuel for heating public buildings' – or as material for the true artist, wearing a moustache and Sam Browne belt. Iconoclasm will often be the word we use to justify our scorning of the idols of a tribe other than our own.

It can be right to fear art; it can also be right to hate and fear iconoclasts. They are often just vandals. It is so easy to wreck what has been painstakingly created. As it was said during the years of persecution in Germany and the Soviet Union, any fool can put a bullet through the head of a genius. The artist Ernst Ludwig Kirchner wrote: 'Events in Germany have deeply shocked me, and yet I am proud that those Brown-shirted iconoclasts are also attacking and destroying my pictures.

I would feel insulted if that kind tolerated me.' Shortly thereafter, he shot himself. Any fool can destroy a work of art. Any fool, for that matter, can mock an art work. Rarely does such mockery amount to anything more than the expression of a kind of aggressive perplexity before the work. Iconoclasts rarely understand the works they assault. Their violence often just proceeds from a fear of the strange or unusual. Tabloid newspaper mockery of new art provides limitless instances of just this kind of stupidity. Indeed, in its worship of the ideal art work (with which the mocked work is tacitly compared) it restates an especially fatuous kind of art idolatry.

And just as one needs to be wary of any uncritical or over-general endorsement of iconoclasm, so one also has to be wary of associating iconoclasm with any specifically Jewish practice. To regard Jews as ironic, corrosive of values, incapable of artistic expression (in the sense of creating works of beauty) is a staple of modern anti-Semitism. This view of the iconoclastic as a kind of Jewish carping – forcing people to reflect, say, on art works that they might prefer to experience uncritically – is what motivated Goebbels to ban art criticism. 'From now on,' he announced on 27 November 1936, 'the reporting of art will take the place of an art criticism which has set itself up as a judge of art – a complete perversion of the concept of criticism which dates from the time of the Jewish domination of art.'

Still, when one separates out what we might term the creative iconoclasm from its destructive alter ego, and distinguishes actual iconoclastic practices from anti-Semitic fantasies, we can see that iconoclastic art is the strongest Jewish art at present. Modern Israeli artists are contributing works to this developing tradition. It is a rigorous art, not for the complacent or those in search of easy pleasures. For quite complex reasons, it tends towards political rather than aesthetic iconoclasm. I am thinking, for example, of what Ofrat terms the radical art of the Territories. Much of it is leftist, and tends to take as its subject what might be described as the idolatry of the land.

More than one route?

These three routes – the aniconic, the iconic, the iconoclastic – are distinct. They represent a choice that modern Jewish artists must make. To attempt more than one has the effect of compromising the artist's work. Or this, at any rate, is the lesson I derive from a study of the work of Grisha Bruskin.

Bruskin (b. 1945) is a Russian-Jewish artist now working in New York. He paints ironic, iconoclastic pictures of the Komar and Melamid type, though without their playfulness or wit. He also paints non-ironic pictures that have as their object the further development of a specifically Jewish iconography. They are positive versions of the ironic pictures. They take the same serial form, but are rich in colour and detail. They have a warmth of engagement that the others altogether lack. Bruskin wants to be both an iconicist and an iconoclast. His works of the first kind are modest successes, the second kind are interesting failures.

First, the iconoclastic. There are two series, *Fundamental Lexicon* and *Logies*. These series comprise paintings which are made up of a potentially infinite number of units or cells, each one of which in turn comprises three elements: figure, object, caption. The figures are grey statues, their expressions comically vacuous; the objects have colour; the captions are enigmatic and weighty. There is an iconostatic effect here. An iconostasis is a screen in an Eastern church which separates the sanctuary from the nave, and on which icons are hung. The screen prevents the laity from witnessing the priests' rituals during services. The Soviet ideology mocked by Bruskin has a parallel effect: it does not reflect, it conceals reality. It is the cover behind which the Party conducts its operations.

The sheer plurality of icons, their obscurity of meaning, the humdrum quality of the objects and the commonplace nature of the figures, their deference to what they hold, all engage with the iconic tradition, but in the register of irony. This is a complex meditation on a tradition in which the artist places himself. He is working to exhaust it. It is as if he is excavating it from within. He will not disclose the living, regal infant. His object is to unveil a gallery of the undead, lacking animating colour or posture. He offers a virtual museum of waxworks. 'My idea,' he says, 'was to create a kind of lexicon of the socialist myth related to the descriptions of idols in the Bible.' Idols, precisely.

But now contrast the *Alephbet* and *Message* series. Four, sometimes five or more, figures, mostly recognizable as Jews, stand in a row, against a backdrop of modern Hebrew script. There are angels too, as well as strange beasts and lettered human forms, and there are symbols (a hand, the moon, flowers and plants, fish, animals). In one of the units in *Alephbet–Lexicon* 7 (1990), there are three Jews and a statue. The first Jew holds a branch with budding leaves, the second Jew wears teffilin (phylacteries), and the third Jew is suspended above the ground by ropes. All three wear the tallith (prayer shawl) and are depicted as celebrating, or suffering for, their faith. The statue I take to be a notionally classical work, and it is crossed out as if to make the point that it represents something that Judaism will not countenance. It has a certain frigid beauty, and it is of course related to the living statues in the *Fundamental Lexicon* and *Logies* series. Worship of Art, worship of the State – both are offensive to the Jewish tradition.

Bruskin has explained: 'Judaism, by virtue of well-known historical reasons, did not create an artistic equivalent to its spiritual initiatives. I always felt a certain cultural vacuum which I thought needed filling in on an individual, artistic level.' And so he fills. He is not satisfied with being an iconoclastic artist. He must also be an iconicist. He must overcome the 'well-known historical reasons' and invent an iconic Jewish art. And he tries to reach the iconic through the iconoclastic: the parallels in design and structure between the two kinds of art are striking, and troubling.

The classical statue in the picture is present 'under erasure' (as we have learned since Derrida to say). It's there, but it's not there. He paints it in order to exclude it; its presence marks its proscription. It represents

62 Grisha Bruskin, *Alephbet–Lexicon 7*, 1990

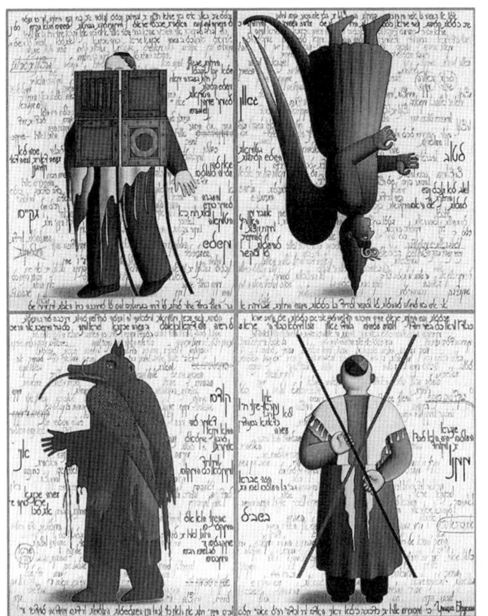

63 Grisha Bruskin, *Message 3*, 1989–90
64 Grisha Bruskin, *Partner*, 1978

a whole project of figuration that is put '*sous rature*'. In *Message 3* (1989–90), a Jewish figure is also represented under erasure, while a second has his face partially obscured. The first one also has his back to us, and appears to be holding the lines that cross him out. It is as if he is participating in his own deletion. He does not wish to be represented.

In a related work, *Partner* (1978), Bruskin has two Jews, one Orthodox and the other secular (actually meant to be the same person, I think, in different garb). The first Jew is solidly supported, both feet squarely on the ground; the second is about to step into thin air, his foot suspended above the void. The Orthodox Jew has his faith; the secular Jew, having abandoned it, has nothing to put in its place. But note the paradox: Bruskin criticizes the secular Jew in a work that could only be painted by another such Jew. This is a figurative work that embraces a religious position that, as the work itself intimates, rejects figuration. The artist has thereby, in a certain sense, put himself too under erasure. This self-cancellation characterizes the project as a whole. It is an art which consists of images that aspire to the condition of language. It is unhappy with itself. Bruskin has created art works that are surrogate books. He cannot resolve the dilemma he has created for himself. While he defers to the Book, and fundamentally to language itself, he also recognizes that, beyond a certain point, this deference must lead to the erasure of his art. So he twists and turns. He gives his art the structure of a book, and puts text in the units, but he then makes the text indecipherable. He gives us the form of words, but they are devoid of communicable content, so that they become images too. This leads to a kind of fetishizing of text, the attributing of magical powers to Hebrew script. To adopt the language of the Christian drama, this is idolatry's last temptation. The Jew, having broken every idol external to his own religious practices, risks being seduced into idolatry of the Torah text.

Bruskin's iconic art is marked by a perpetual irresolution. What he wants to paint he must erase, and what he doesn't want to paint he must present. What Bruskin wants to write he must picture, and what he wants to picture, he must scribble, unintelligibly. This leads to a kind of aporetic indecisiveness – to write or to picture?; to present or to erase? – which has as its consequence an endless repetition, as if the repetition in itself would solve the dilemma. And in this respect, the open-endedness of the two Jewish series is quite different to that of the two Soviet series. *Fundamental Lexicon* and *Logies* are open-ended because the Soviet system has no regard for the individuality of human beings, who are thus endlessly reproduced, without distinguishing colour, as grey as unpainted toy soldiers turned out by factory machines. *Alephbet* and *Messages* are open-ended because Bruskin just can't help it.

Of course, there is a sense in which idolizing and iconoclastic art works will always court their own extinction. Idolizing works will do so because they efface themselves before the greater reality of their subject (the god, the monarch). Iconoclastic works will do so because they undo themselves by simultaneously representing and cancelling their subject (the god, the monarch).

There is, in truth, a triviality about the pictures in Bruskin's two Jewish series. They even convey – dare I say it? – a certain 'wallpaper' effect. While the units are lovely to look at, they are unlikely ever to disturb or enlarge the imagination. Such art has an unlimited future (Bruskin has introduced a third series, *Metamorphoses*). I do not want to be over-rigorous, and I think some of his sculptural works are rather fine. But for those of us who would wish for another kind of Jewish art – an iconoclastic one, which must actively promote, while creatively deferring, its own extinction – Bruskin's essentially decorative art is slightly depressing.

Jewish creativity

There is a risk that the search for a Jewish art will lead to a certain fetishism: isolating one aspect in a number of works and then mistaking it as constitutive of them. Such an endeavour, which by implication assumes the self-sufficiency of ethnicity, has a quality of the idolatrous about it. Can a theory of Jewish art avoid the idolatry of Jewishness? Only if it is modest, and takes care. It must concede that the art works it describes as Jewish may also be described in other ways too. A Jewish art work will never be exclusively Jewish; it will always also be of a particular style and period. Consider Jacob Kramer's *Day of Atonement* (1919): notwithstanding both its subject and its author, its Jewish qualities are among the least significant aspects of this work. And even Joshua Neustein, of whom Kampf triumphantly says that he 'surrenders nothing of his Jewish self-possession in order to be an American or Israeli artist,' is deeply indebted to a post-Duchampian conceptualism on which he merely plays a series of variations.

A theory of Jewish art must also acknowledge that the very notion 'Jewish art' is not susceptible to any very precise definition. People who use it often want to include much, though by no means all, art made by Jews. They often also want to include art made by non-Jews for a Jewish

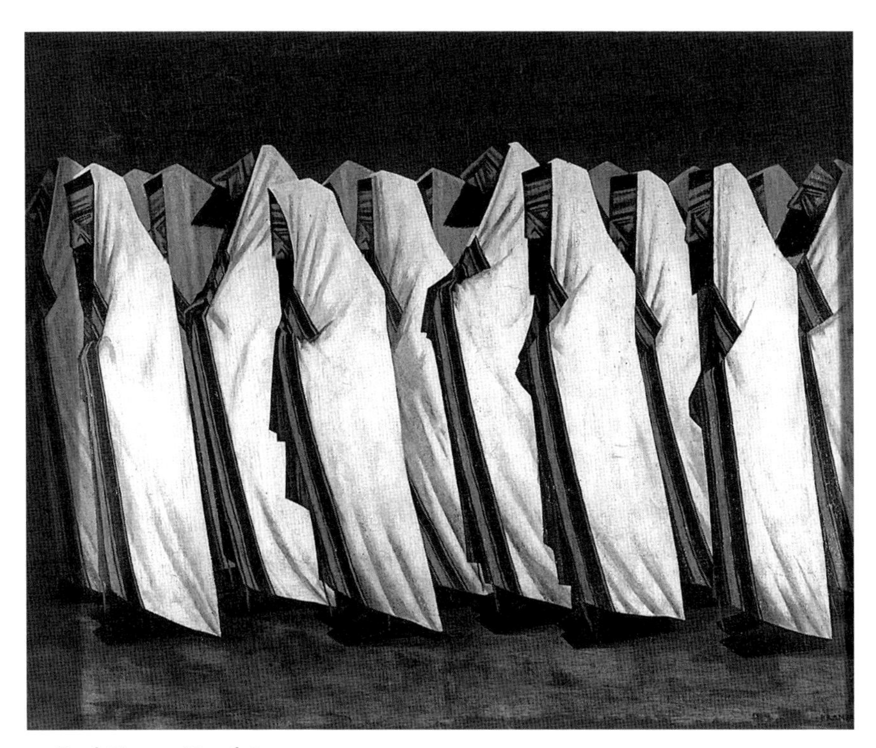

65 Jacob Kramer, *Day of Atonement*, 1919

purpose (decorating a synagogue, supporting a ritual) or with a Jewish subject. They do not, in the main, take too seriously the prohibitions, even though this leads to the somewhat paradoxical understanding of Jewish art as an art which violates Jewish law. And they wrestle with Israeli art, often for related reasons. Consider, for example, Itzhak Danziger's *Nimrod* (1939). Its rejection of Jewish values is categoric; Danziger was one of a group of artists who considered themselves to be 'Canaanites' and sought to return to the country's pre-Jewish origins. Nimrod was an idolator and a false deity, the builder of the tower of Babel and the persecutor of Abraham. Hence the dilemma: given the work's nature, how can it be Jewish art?; but given its authorship, how can it not?

There will thus always be disagreement on what to include (is there a kind of art which is Jewish by the nature of its blasphemy, for

66 Itzhak Danziger, *Nimrod*, 1939

example?), and no theory of Jewish art will quite be able to adjudicate on difficult, marginal works. How, indeed, could this be otherwise when art works that are either by, or for, or about Jews are all candidates? But for a non-idolatrous theory of Jewish art none of this matters in the least. From time to time in Jewish history, hopes have been nursed of what has been described as a utopia of isolation and exclusivity, where Jewish culture would contain everything needed by Jewish artists for their art. Nothing would need to be borrowed; everything would be drawn from a Jewish source. These hopes have not been realized, not least because they cannot be realized.

It follows that Jewish art is a porous and non-exclusive category. Few art works will ever be incontestably Jewish; no art will ever be merely or entirely Jewish. Yet for all this, the concept of Jewish art is not wholly useless. It has some explanatory value. It can disclose affiliations and meanings in art works that might otherwise escape notice. It also has an aspirational value. It encourages the making of new art works by providing a context for them. It gives the artist a history (however modest) within which he can work, an iconography (more modest still) on which he can draw, and a canon (modest, but growing) to which he can contribute.

Understood in this way, the concept of Jewish art administers a proper rebuke to four kinds of art critic. There are the critics who would deny that Jews have any aptitude for the visual arts. These critics assume the burden of explaining what they believe to be the absence of Jewish art. The anti-Semitic explanation denies Jewish creativity altogether; another explanation holds Jewish creativity to be aural rather than visual, and to be more sensitive to time than space. The prohibition of any surrender to 'the distinctive form-producing values of art', Weber argued, limited Jewish artistic expression. Herbert Read proposed that the continuing paucity of Jewish art was attributable to the nomadic origins of the Jews. One response by Jewish critics to this argument has been to concede the absence of art during the period that the Jews were nomadic, but to insist that a vital and flourishing Jewish art came into existence once Jews started building, and settling in, cities. Joseph Gutmann, for example, attributed the Second Commandment itself to the Jews' initially semi-nomadic life.

And then there are the critics who would dissolve the concept of Jewish art in the larger one of a universal art. Too much talk of Jewish art can have a cramping effect on the Jewish artist's creativity. Ethnic particularism is to be deprecated; the sooner Jews emancipate themselves from their local loyalties, the better their art will become. In a little essay, 'What is Jewish Art?', Chagall was optimistic about the Jewish contribution to art, and indifferent about whether it would be distinctively Jewish. Christian Boltanski likewise says: '[my work] is post-Holocaust art, but that is not the same as saying that it is Jewish art. I hope my work is general.' The Russian avant-gardiste El Lissitsky started his career promoting Jewish national art but then abandoned Jewish themes in favour of a universal language of abstraction. The Israeli artist Yossef Zaritsky believed that the future of Israeli art lay in adopting what he regarded as contemporary art's universal language. Boltanski is probably right about his own work, Chagall probably wrong about *his* work. Lissitsky did not quite escape his early ambitions; Zaritsky's plans for Israeli art were indicative of a certain lack of cultural self-confidence. But the universalist critic is not interested in such discriminations. Jews have always struggled with the tension between the universal and the particular in their faith. It is perhaps only in the emphatic nature of his insistence upon the universal character of art, one which expresses itself in a quest for that one representation which unifies all human experience, that Rothko discloses himself as a painter of Jewish origins.

Third, there are the postmodernist critics for whom the concept 'Jewish' is a construction, to be deconstructed. They would dissolve *all* concepts; for them, the 'universal' is the most bogus concept of all. Juliet Steyn's *The Jew: Assumptions of Identity* (London, 1999) takes just this position. She wishes, she explains, to dismantle 'the subject'. She regards the concept of identity as a provocation. We know, she says, what happens when 'the Jew' has been catalogued. The truth, she insists, is that Jews are 'a group without a single foundation, a heterogeneous linkage of the non-identical.' Jews who think otherwise are mistaken, she implies. But our misconceptions about who we are form part of who we are. They are the mistakes, so to speak, which we live. Kitaj gets it right, I think, when he writes, first: 'the still hotly debated question – What is a Jew? – has never been resolved, except perhaps by murderers,' but then second: 'the trouble with Jews is that we are an endangered nation, almost always.' In other words, for all that, there *is* a 'we'. This is perhaps a reflex of Jewish artists. The reflex is evident, in a slightly different manner, in some remarks made by Mark Gertler. On the one hand, he could say: 'I shall be free and detached ... I shall be neither Jew nor Christian ... I shall just be myself and be able to work out things according to my own tastes.' But on the other hand he could also say: 'as far as Jewish art is concerned, I do not think that we have yet distinguished ourselves as much as we could do.'

And last, there are the critics who, as a rejoinder to the anti-Semites, narrate the story of Jewish art as a tale of triumphs. They are motivated by a desire to give comfort and pride to their co-religionists and to confound their mutual enemies. These are the Jewish apologists. Cecil Roth is chief among them. His *Jewish Art: An Illustrated History* (Jerusalem, 1971) sets out to celebrate 'the artistic achievements in every medium of Jews and persons of Jewish birth.' This is of a piece with those many books in which Jews are hailed as good at most things. Their contributions to science, music, philosophy, literature, are all recorded with an anxious pride. Listing Jewish Nobel laureates, for example, became standard in the many books of the 1930s written to counter anti-Semitism (as if evidence of one's talent could win around one's enemies). The great Judaica collection at the Smithsonian was assembled by Cyrus Adler for the precise purpose of countering anti-Semitism and helping secure the place of Jews in American society. The Bezalel Art Institute in Jerusalem was established in 1906 with the aim of inspiring Jewish creativity and instilling pride in Jewish artistic achievements. The collection would in due course comprise, the founder Boris Schatz hoped, a 'Jewish pantheon'.

The conception of Jewish art I have tried to develop is distinct (in certain respects, counter) to each one of the above. But it too, in due course, will have to give way before new works that trespass its boundaries. There is already a new art which responds to what Kitaj has described as 'a rumour of Jewishness'. I have in mind, for example, the work of Christian Boltanski. In the end, art will always elude the systematizers.

Bibliographical essay

ABRAHAM WAS THE FIRST JEWISH ICONOCLAST. His idol-breaking activities, which of course precede the giving of the Ten Commandments, are only hinted at in Genesis. James L. Kugel *The Bible As It Was* (Cambridge, Mass., 1997) explains how this hint was developed by early commentators, and Louis Ginzberg *The Legends of the Jews* (Baltimore, 1998) summarizes their stories. The Talmudic tractate *Avodah Zara* (London, 1988) concerns the laws relating to strange or alien worship, and tractates *Rosh Hashanah* (London, 1990) and *Shabbos* (London, 1987) also contain passages on idolatry. Nachmanides *Commentaries on the Torah* (New York, 1973) contains important glosses on Exodus XX and Deuteronomy IV. Maimonides *Hilchot Avodat Kochavin V'Chukkoteihem* (Jerusalem, 1990) is a statement of the law on idolatry, and his *Moreh Nebuchim* (or *Guide for the Perplexed*) (London, 1904) contains a number of passages on the same subject. David Hartman *A Living Covenant* (Woodstock, 1997) is an account of modern Orthodox Judaism which pays particular attention, from an essentially Maimonidean perspective, to the question of idolatry. Josef Stern *Problems and Parables of Law* (New York, 1998) considers the implications of Maimonides' acknowledgment of the formative role of pagan myths on the rituals and commandments of the Mosaic Law.

I took the passage about the obligation to destroy idols from Samson Raphael Hirsch *Horeb* (New York, 1962; first published in 1837). Hirsch regards as idolatrous the treating of any person or element in Nature or Society as acting by its own power or will (see Section 1, ch. 3). Franz Rosenzweig's characterization of the artist is to be found in *The Star of Redemption* (London, 1971); his characterization of the state and art as the eternal gods of paganism is quoted in Robert Gibbs *Correlations in Rosenzweig and Levinas* (Princeton, 1992). The quotations from Josephus are taken from his essay 'Against Apion', in *The Works of Josephus* (London, 1818). Apion was an anti-Semite whose opinions about the Jews are preserved in the medium of Josephus' refutations. My summary of Levinas follows a reading of his essay 'Reality and its Shadow', in *The Levinas Reader* (Oxford, 1989), ed. Sean Hand (though I also took a sentence from an interview quoted in Judith Friedlander *Vilna on the Seine* [New

Haven, 1990]). His conclusion is the familiar one that 'the proscription of images is truly the supreme command of monotheism.' The suggestion that Christianity needs art 'to seduce and subdue' the convert from paganism is made in his essay 'Franz Rosenzweig: A Modern Jewish Thinker', in *Outside the Subject* (London, 1993). The quotation from Soloveitchik may be found in *Halakhic Man* (Philadelphia, 1983). The Adorno quotation is from *Aesthetic Theory* (London, 1986). The reference to 'impious Jews' is taken from John G. Gager *The Origins of Anti-Semitism* (New York, 1985). On the distinctness of Jewish Messianism, I read Gershom Scholem *The Messianic Idea in Judaism* (New York, 1971), from which I took the Maimonides quotation, and where I found R. Israel of Rizhin's views summarized.

Idolatry (Cambridge, Mass., 1992) by Moshe Halbertal and Avishai Margalit is a magisterial account of the topic written from within a Jewish perspective. I took from it my characterization of philosophy as iconoclastic, as well as the quotation from Wittgenstein. They define idolatry as 'any nonabsolute value that is made absolute and demands to be the centre of dedicated life.' I likewise learned a great deal from Lionel Kochan's *Beyond the Graven Image: A Jewish View* (New York, 1997), which contains Rosenzweig's 'anti-religion' remark, and which develops the notion of a Bezalelian 'art in the shade'. I have taken from Kochan's *Jews, Idols and Messiahs* (Oxford, 1990) the art/monotheism antithesis. The unnamed Jewish sage is Hermann Cohen. Kochan relates Cohen's remark to a passage in *The Essence of Christianity* (New York, 1957) where Feuerbach argues that while both science and art derive from polytheism, Jewish monotheism is pure egotism and has itself as its end. Kochan offers no comment, although I think one is needed. Feuerbach's version of the antithesis is surely one further instance of the hostile spin that anti-Semites characteristically seek to put on the complex distinctness of Judaism.

There is a chapter in Emil Fackenheim's *Encounters between Judaism and Modern Philosophy* (New York, 1980), 'Idolatry as a Modern Possibility', which relates ancient to modern forms of idolatry and from which I have taken my Luther, Barth and Tillich quotations. Luther hints, incidentally, in his *Table Talk* (London, 1995), that he understands the tribal aspect of idolatry. Are not Protestants open to the very charge of idolatry that we lay against Catholics? But then he retreats: 'we that truly believe in Christ, and are of his mind, we ... know and judge all things, but are judged of no human creature.' The contemporary Protestant theologian Hans Kung praises Judaism for the rigour of its monotheistic repudiation of idolatry: 'it means the radical repudiation of the many gods who nowadays are worshipped by men and women without any divine title: of all earthly entities with a divine function, on who a person may feel that everyone depends ... it gives great freedom, because it relativizes all the other powers and authorities in the world which so easily enslave people...', *Judaism* (London, 1992).

Leon Roth *Is There a Jewish Philosophy?* (London, 1999) likewise relates the ancient prohibition against idolatry to modern passions (and is also my source for the characterization of Judaism as the depopulator of the heavens). Ernst Cassirer discusses political idolatry in *The Myth of the State* (New Haven, 1946). The Heidegger quotation is in Robert S. Wistrich *Weekend in Munich: Art, Propaganda and Terror in the Third Reich* (London, 1995). Cynthia Ozick's 'Literature as Idol: Harold Bloom' (in *Art and Ardor* [New York, 1984]) continues the Jewish labour of idol-breaking, and is a marvellous rejoinder to Bloom's self-understanding as a Jewish Gnostic. In the absence of the Second Commandment, she says, idolatry will always be reconstituted – if not in wood or stone, then in philosophical or political concept; if not in philosophical or political concept, then in literature. The collection of critical essays on Ozick edited by Bloom, *Cynthia Ozick: Modern Critical Views* (New York, 1986), contains his slightly feeble rejoinder. He argues that she is a self-deceiving critic, and a writer who trusts only in the covenant between her stories and other people's stories.

R. Shlomo Ganzfried *Kitzur Shulchan Aruch* (New York, 1992; first published in 1864), chs 167–68, purports to be authoritative on what Jewish artists are allowed to do. (While Ganzfried's work is an abridgment of Joseph Karo's 16th-century *Shulchan Aruch*, the authoritative codification of Jewish law, it does draw out the implications in the latter's proscriptions in the matter of art and sculpture – I am grateful to Marcel Borden for clarifying this for me, as well as for being an early, challenging audience for some of the ideas in this book.) Though I have given the *Kitzur* as my reference for the statement that Jews have a duty to mock idolatry, it appears first in the Talmudic tractates *Megillah* and *Sanhedrin*. Steven Schwarzschild's 'The Legal Foundations of Jewish Aesthetics' in *The Pursuit of the Ideal*, ed. M. Kellner (New York, 1990), relates one aspect of Jewish aniconicism to modern art, and overstates (by a long way) the Jewish nature of that art. While *Jewish Identity in Modern Art History*, ed. Catherine M. Soussloff, contains a number of very good essays, I learned most from Kalman P. Bland's 'Anti-Semitism and Aniconicism' and Lisa Saltzman's 'To Figure or Not to Figure'. I am grateful to Grace Cohen Grossman for sending to me Joseph Gutmann's 'The Second Commandment and the Image in Judaism', which is an essay in a book edited by him, *No Graven Images* (New York, 1971). He hears Platonic echoes in

Philo's animadversions against painting and sculpture, and he sees only obstacles to art in the Second Commandment. Jacques Aumant's *The Image* (London, 1997) arrives at the Jewish conclusion that while 'the massive multiplication of images may appear to signal a return of the image ... our civilisation remains ... a civilisation of language.' James Fenton's essay 'On Statues', in *Leonardo's Nephew* (London, 1999), also engages – engagingly – with a number of these ideas. My authority for the proposition that distorted representations of human likenesses are permitted in Jewish law is the *Kitzur Shulchan Aruch*, which provides: 'It is ... forbidden to sculpture an image of a person. Even the face of a person is prohibited.... However, only a full face is forbidden, that is, when it has two eyes and a complete nose, but if it is only half a face, a profile ... that is not forbidden.'

On the ideology/idolatry nexus, Halbertal and Margalit started me off. Michael Rosen's *On Voluntary Servitude: False Consciousness and the Theory of Ideology* (Oxford, 1996) is the most sophisticated modern account of ideology that I know. The chant 'no images, no Papists' is quoted by Christopher Hill in *Milton and the English Revolution* (London, 1997). Louis Althusser's 'Ideology and Ideological State Apparatuses (Notes Towards an Investigation)' in *Lenin and Philosophy* (London, 1977) states the terminal point I describe at the end of my paragraph; the quotation from Althusser comes from another essay in the same book, 'Cremoni, Painter of the Abstract'.

As for the theory of the icon, my starting point was Victor Y. Bychkov's authoritative and succinct article 'Icon' in *Encyclopedia of Aesthetics* (New York, 1998), ed. Michael Kelly. The icon's 'spiritual, sacred, corporeity' is Sergij Bulgakov's characterization, which Bychkov quotes. Moshe Barasch *Icon* (New York, 1995) is a thorough account of the doctrine of the image from an art-historical perspective. Engelina Smirnova *Moscow Icons: 14th–17th Centuries* (Leningrad, 1989) contains many reproductions of icons. The understanding of icons as *acheiropoieta* is a point made by Julian Bell in *What is Painting?* (London, 1999). He sets the 'Platonic and Judaic' rejection of images against the Aristotelian and Christian embracing of them. 'The battle between these two viewpoints,' he argues, 'has continued to this day.' There is, I can see, a tendency in my own book to find only battles, or differences, between Judaism and Christianity. For a corrective to this tendency, I refer the reader to Daniel Boyarin *Dying for God* (Stanford, 1999), which represents the two as 'complexly related subsystems of one religious polysystem.'

I came to W. J. T. Mitchell's *Iconology* (Chicago, 1986) quite late on, after I had finished the first draft of this book. It is an immensely impressive and comprehensive examination of the ideology of the image. But Mitchell elides the Jewish and the Protestant critique of idolatry, and overlooks the Incarnation when he writes of the 'invisible god of the Judeo-Christian tradition.' It was Leonardo da Vinci who characterized the idolator as a person who demands help from the idol. I took this from Mitchell, who quotes the artist: 'If you, poet, describe the figure of some deities, the writing will not be held in the same veneration as the painted deity, because bows and various prayers will continually be made to the painting. To it will throng many generations from many provinces and from over the eastern seas, and they will demand help from the painting and not from what is written.'

I discovered the Ingres picture in Stephen F. Eisenman's survey *Nineteenth-Century Art: A Critical Introduction* (London and New York, 1994), where Thomas Crow's discussion of it (pp. 73–74) set me thinking about some of the themes that inform this short book. Crow says that the vow in question was a dedication of the kingdom to the Virgin in an appeal for divine assistance in defeating the forces of the French Protestants. Elizabeth Gilmore Holt, in a footnote to Stendhal's article on *The Vow*, says that it commemorates the king's gratitude for intercession when the French army forced passage through La Brunette, a pass into Italy, and defeated the Duke of Savoy, in March 1629: see *The Triumph of Art for the Public 1785–1848* (Princeton, 1979). Ernst Gombrich writes about the evolution in the art of the altarpiece in *The Uses of Images* (London, 1999), and Lisa Jardine writes about the authority of the altarpiece in *Worldly Goods* (London, 1996).

Robert Rosenblum's monograph *Ingres* (London, 1985) is authoritative. Jon Whitely's *Ingres* (London, 1977) added some helpful details, and I have drawn from it my account of the commissioning of *The Vow*. The judgment regarding Ingres' standing among conservatives comes from Walter Friedlander *David to Delacroix* (Cambridge, Mass., 1952). (For an account of Ingres' work which registers its political complexity, see Adrian Rifkin *Ingres Then, and Now* [London, 2000], which also is sharp-eyed about the carpet in *Napoleon*.) Friedlander remarks that Ingres 'objected violently to being counted simply as a slavish imitator of his idolized Raphael.' The art book that describes Raphael as Ingres' idol is *The Art Book* (London, 1994). I have borrowed from Patricia Mainardi's *The End of the Salon: Art and the State in the Early Third Republic* (Cambridge, 1993) the 'throne and altar' characterization of Ingres' art. Carol Duncan's 'Ingres' *Vow of Louis XIII* and the Politics of the Restoration', in *The Aesthetics of Power* (Cambridge, 1993), gives a very full account of the picture's origins and political context (and thanks to Tamar Garb for sending it to me). She doesn't like the picture much. (For an account of the picture which is very different from my own, see Richard Wollheim, *Painting as an Art* [London, 1987].) The quotation from Ingres comes from Charles Rosen and Henri Zerner *Romanticism and Realism: The Mythology of Nineteenth Century Art* (London, 1984). The quotation from Baudelaire comes from 'Salon de 1845' in the Pléiade edition of the *Oeuvres Complètes* (Paris, 1971). The Gautier quotation comes from Gene H. Bell-Villada *Art for Art's Sake and Literary Life* (Lincoln, 1996).

For Raphael, I have relied on Konrad Oberhuber *Raphael: The Paintings* (Munich, 1999). Incidentally, he considers *La Fornarina* to be Raphael's, although it was possibly unfinished at his death. Robert Rosenblum, by contrast, regards the work to be by Raphael's pupil, Giulio Romano.

The Ghiberti passage, which is taken from the second of his *Commentarii*, is translated and abridged in *A Documentary History of Art*, Vol. 1, ed. Elizabeth Gilmore Holt (Princeton, 1947). Moshe Barasch *Theories of Art: From Plato to Winkelmann* (New York, 1985) finds in Horace an example of the sophisticated pagan contempt for idolatry: 'Once upon a time I was the trunk of a wild fig-tree, a useless log, when a carpenter, after some doubt as to whether to make me a privy or a Priapus, decided to make me into a god.' Barasch argues that early Christian attitudes towards art were indebted to this pagan scepticism. The Augustine passage comes from Book IV, chs 31 and 34, *The City of God* (London, 1972). He is quite clear about the causes of the Jews' misfortunes: 'if [the Jews] had not sinned against God by turning aside to the worship of strange gods and of idols, seduced by impious superstition as if by magic arts, if they had not finally sinned by putting Christ to death, they would have continued in possession of the same realm, a realm exceeding others in happiness, if not in extent.' Their dispersal, he adds, is proof to idolators of the providence of the one true God. St Luke's career as a painter is considered in James Hall *The World as Sculpture* (London, 1999). The Hegel quotation may be found in Vol. 1, section III, ch. I of his *Aesthetics* (Oxford, 1975). The quotation from *Mediator Dei* is taken from Edgar Wind, 'Traditional Religion and Modern Art', *The Eloquence of Symbols* (Oxford, 1993).

I first came across Komar and Melamid's *Origins of Socialist Realism* in Edward Lucie-Smith's *Art Today* (London, 1995). I found the *Post Art* pictures in *Komar/Melamid: Two Soviet Dissident Artists*, ed. Melvyn B. Nathanson (Illinois, 1979). The exhibition catalogue for *Monumental Propaganda*, which was published in 1993 in New York, contains the Komar and Melamid open letters and their essay 'We Remember,

Or So It Seems' (from which the reference to 'the land of mummies and pyramids' is taken). *Painting by Numbers: Komar and Melamid's Scientific Guide to Art*, ed. JoAnn Wypijewski (Berkeley, 1999) is also an exhibition catalogue of sorts, and accompanied the Komar and Melamid roadshow (there is another catalogue containing the 'Most Wanted' art which adds further instances, including *The Web's Least Wanted Painting* and *The Web's Most Wanted Painting*: Komar and Melamid *The Most Wanted and Most Unwanted Painting* [Ostfildern-Ruit, 1997]). They toured museums with their 'Most Wanted' and 'Most Unwanted' pictures and held public meetings where the pictures were debated. There is a very good essay by Arthur Danto in the catalogue, which asks: can it be the 'Most Wanted Painting' even if nobody wants it? I should add that I find Komar and Melamid's surprise about the appeal of blue landscapes to be itself slightly surprising. Kandinsky explained it fully, just under a century ago. 'Blue,' he wrote, 'is the typical heavenly colour. The ultimate feeling it creates is one of rest...' (see *Concerning the Spiritual in Art* [New York, 1977]).

I have not been able to get hold of *A. Ziablov* and so I have had to rely on the extracts and summary in Boris Groys *The Total Art of Stalinism* (New Jersey, 1992). Groys' book, incidentally, is praised by Komar and Melamid in their interview in the *Painting by Numbers* catalogue. The quotation from Komar about the 'old gods' comes from Valerie Hillings' 'Komar and Melamid's Dialogue with (Art) History' in *art journal* (Winter 1999), and she in turn got it from David Remnick, 'What Becomes a Lenin Most', *Washington Post*, 25 July 1993. The quotation from the Komar and Melamid interview at the end of the *Art Iconoclasm* section comes from Renee Baigell and Matthew Baigell *Soviet Dissident Artists: Interviews after Perestroika* (New Brunswick, 1995). It is Andrew Roberts who says that the joke is on the people, and he says it in 'Poll Stars', *Artforum* (January 1995). The quotation from Lenin comes from Edward Lucie-Smith's contribution to *Index on Censorship* 6/1999 (and thank you Dan Jacobson for sending this volume to me). My brief discussion of the nature of irony owes much to Alexander Nehemas *The Art of Living* (Berkeley, 2000) and Richard Rorty *Contingency, Irony and Solidarity* (Cambridge, 1989). N. Sokolow's essay 'Irony', *An Anthology of Hebrew Essays* (Tel Aviv, 1966), selected by I. Cohen and B.Y. Michali, treats irony as the principal weapon available to Jews against idolatries that threaten them. I have taken my Midrash quotation from Emil Fackenheim *What is Judaism?* (New York, 1987). It was in Julian Bell *What is Painting?* (op. cit.) that I first saw the David Allan picture, and in David Carrier *Artwriting* (Amherst, 1987) that I found the connection made between Pliny and Komar and Melamid. Leo Steinberg

The Sexuality of Christ in Renaissance Art and in Modern Oblivion (Chicago, 1996; 2nd ed.) is my source for the material relating to 'chin-chucking'.

For Unofficial Art in general, I consulted: *Forbidden Art: the Postwar Russian Avant-Garde* (New York, 1998), a particularly substantial exhibition catalogue with a useful chronology, detailed artists' biographies and several outstanding essays (including one by Yevgeni Barabanov which quotes Grobman, and one by Karl Eimermacher which quotes the clerical ideologist whom I have in turn quoted); Alla Rosenfeld and Norton T. Dodge *Nonconformist Art: the Soviet Experience 1956–1986* (London, 1995), which introduces the private collection of Mr Dodge, an economics professor in the United States, and also contains some very good essays; Matthew Cullerne Bown *Contemporary Russian Art* (London, 1989); Ekaterina Andreeva *Sots Art: Soviet Artists of the 1970s and 1980s* (Roseville East, 1995); and Andrew Solomon *The Irony Tower* (New York, 1991), which is particularly interesting on Shvartsman, and says of Bruskin: 'His work is explicitly political, or else it is explicitly concerned with his Judaism. His images are haunting, like the images of advertizing....'

As for Malevich, Rainer Crone and David Moos *Kazimir Malevich* (London, 1991) is just excellent. Malevich's *From Cubism to Suprematism* is in *Russian Art of the Avant Garde*, ed. John E. Bowlt (London, 1988). The account of the hanging of *Black Square* I took from Bruce Altshuler *The Avant-Garde in Exhibition: New Art in the 20th Century* (Berkeley, 1994).

On Socialist Realism, the books that I found most helpful were the following: Igor Golomstock *Totalitarian Art* (London, 1990), though it tries too hard, I think, to assimilate Soviet, Third Reich, Italian Fascist and Maoist Chinese art to a single form (the Nazi references come from this book); Boris Groys (op. cit.), though it tries too hard to implicate the avant-garde in its indictment of Stalin and Socialist Realism; and Matthew Cullerne Bown *Socialist Realist Painting* (New Haven, 1998), which, by contrast, attends scrupulously to the specificity of the Socialist Realist art form.

Among the surveys on Jewish art I consulted were: first and foremost, Gabrielle Sed-Rayna *Jewish Art* (New York, 1997), on which I have relied for my account of Antokolsky; Avram Kampf *Chagall to Kitaj: Jewish Experience in 20th-Century Art* (London, 1990), from which I took the Tchernichovski poem, the quotations from Kitaj, from Ardon, and the Jewish critic who comments on Jews and art; Helen Rosenau *A Short History of Jewish Art* (London, 1948) which concludes that the history of Jewish art is one of painting and architecture, and not sculpture; Irene Korn *A Celebration of Judaism in Art* (New York, 1996), which usefully brings together many examples of pictures that take as their subject aspects of Jewish practice; Ernest Namenyi *The Essence of Jewish Art* (New York, 1957); *Russian-Jewish Artists in a Century of Change 1890-1990* ed. Susan Tumarkin Goodman (Munich, 1995); *Jewish Artists: The Ben Uri Collection* (London, 1987), ed. W.M. Schwab, from which I took the Hart anecdote; and Grace Cohen Grossman (with Richard Eighme Ahlborn) *Judaica at the Smithsonian* (Washington, D.C., 1997), which catalogues and contextualizes an exceptionally impressive collection. Ellen S. Saltman's 'The Forbidden Image in Jewish Art' (*Journal of Jewish Art* Vol. 8, 1981) identifies the very rare number of representations of the Divine in Jewish art. Charles Spencer – whose opinion I quote on the impairing effect of the prohibitions – jokes about the 'Cecil-Roth-*nachus*-syndrome' in 'Towards a Definition of Jewish Art' *Jewish Perspectives* (London, 1980), ed. Jacob Sontag.

On Holocaust art, I consulted: Ziva Amishai-Maisels *Depiction and Interpretation: The Influence of the Holocaust on the Visual Arts* (Oxford, 1993), from which I took the Konieczny quotation; *After Auschwitz*, ed. Monica Bohm-Duchen (London, 1995), which is where I learned of Chagall's original title for *Liberation* (Bohm-Duchen commends Kitaj for finding in the crematorium chimney the Jewish equivalent of the cross); *Witness & Legacy: Contemporary Art about the Holocaust* (Minneapolis, 1995), an exhibition catalogue of art works that address the Holocaust, ed. Stephen C. Feinstein; Janet Blatter and Sybil Milton *Art of the Holocaust* (London, 1982 – and thanks to my mother Myrna Julius for lending it to me). Yigal Zalmona's commentary on the Israel Museum's modern art collection ('The Art Collections', *The Israel Museum* [Tel Aviv, 1995]) was particularly helpful on Danziger, Lissitsky and Zaritsky.

Rachel Wischnitzer's 'Judaism and Art', in *The Jews: Their Role in Civilization* (New York, 1971) contends that Impressionism, and by implication Modernism and all art thereafter, gave up 'art's claim to divinity and exclusiveness', a renunciation that then allowed Jews to become artists. This essay, and Harold Rosenberg's 'Jews in Art', in *Art and Other Serious Matters* (Chicago, 1985), comprised a stimulating counter to my own thinking about whether one can usefully describe an art work as 'Jewish'. I took from Richard I. Cohen's magisterial *Jewish Icons: Art and Society in Modern Europe* (Berkeley, 1998) the quotation from Graetz; the mention of the Rabbinical portrait; and the reference to the Bezalel Art Institute. I refer to the ample evidence in Heinz Schreckenberg *The Jews in Christian Art* (New York, 1996) to support my characterization of Christian art as hostile to Jews. Michael Berkowitz's wonderfully scholarly and enjoyable *The Jewish Self-Image* (London, 2000) discusses many modern Jewish 'icons'.

The allegedly repressed Jewishness of Soutine's work is advanced as a thesis by Maurice Tuchman (as summarized by Kampf, op. cit.): '[Soutine's] preoccupation with animals and food was a symbolic violation of Jewish law, and his stress on the importance of concretely conceived objections a reaction to the visual prohibitions of Jewish doctrine deeply honoured in the shtetl.' Peter Fuller agrees (though with an uncertain grasp of the specifics of Jewish law): 'He would string up a flayed ox in the studio, and paint in a frenzy in front of it. The terror of the act for him might have been intensified by the fact that he thereby violated Jewish laws about the handling of flesh and blood.' However, Fuller adds – and this is what is important – that Soutine's work evinces a 'sense of continuity with the art of Rembrandt, Goya, Courbet and, behind them, the wealth of a Christian iconography of redeemed sacrifice' (*Images of God* [London, 1990]).

I also consulted the following non-art books for what they had to say about Jewish art: Cecil Roth *The Jews in the Renaissance* (Philadelphia, 1959), for the remark about Jewish painters and Christian art, and for the 'liberal' vs 'literal' reading of the Second Commandment; Marcel Simon *Verus Israel* (London, 1986), for the art of Palestinian Judaism (which also invokes the 'Rabbinic liberalism' doctrine, restated by Rabbi Louis Jacobs in the entry 'Art' in *The Jewish Religion: A Companion* [Oxford, 1995]); Irving Howe *The Immigrant Jews on New York 1881 to the Present* (London, 1976), from which I have taken the Maurice Sterne anecdote; and the multi-volume *Encyclopedia Judaica* (Jerusalem, n.d.), an invaluable resource. Rosenzweig's erroneous claim about synagogue art is made in *Judaism Despite Christianity* (New York, 1971), his collected correspondence with the Christian theologian Eugen Rosenstock-Huessy. Max Weber makes his remarks about Judaism's (and Puritanism's) 'rejection of all distinctively aesthetic devices' in *The Sociology of Religion* (London, 1965).

The Ahad Ha-Am essay 'The Question of Jewish Culture' is anthologized in *Contemporary Jewish Thought: A Reader* ed. Simon Noveck (Washington D.C., 1972). He was a little hard on Antokolsky (who had in his life more than enough trouble from anti-Semites); he made art works with Jewish themes, though it is true that he did not appear to regard his vocation as that of a Jewish artist. It is in Leo Kenig's essay 'Jewish Art' (*Great Yiddish Writers of the Twentieth Century*, selected and translated by Joseph Leftwich [New Jersey and London, 1969]) that the claim that modern art is especially congenial to Jews may be found. The medieval poem (by Rabbenu Gershom) is taken from Jacob Katz, *Exclusiveness and Tolerance* (New York, 1962). The Gertler quotations come from John Woodeson *Mark Gertler* (London, 1972), and thank you

Frances Gertler for lending the book to me. The 'utopia of isolation and exclusivity' is considered in Yaacov Shavit *Athens in Jerusalem: Classical Antiquity and Hellenism in the Making of the Modern Secular Jew* (London, 1997).

My thinking about the sublime relies on Kant's *Critique of Judgment* (Oxford, 1973). His reference to the Second Commandment may be found in Book II, 'General Remark on the Exposition of Aesthetic Reflective Judgments'. Kant's point about the interdependence of the religious and the political was made in a less philosophical context by Bishop Gardiner when he warned Henry VIII that the destruction of religious images would weaken respect for the coats of arms of the nobility and even for the royal arms (see Hill, op. cit.). In contrast, Diarmaid MacCulloch *Tudor Church Militant: Edward VI and the Protestant Reformation* (London, 1999) draws attention to the common identification of Edward with the Biblical king Josiah, both of them boy-kings who purged their land of idols.

The Lyotard essay 'Answering the Question: What is Postmodernism?' is the appendix to *The Postmodern Condition: A Report on Knowledge* (Manchester, 1989). I also found helpful Phillipe Lacoue-Labarthe's essay 'Sublime Truth' in *Of the Sublime: Presence in Question* (New York, 1993). He describes the iconoclastic prescription as a 'meta-sublime statement' because 'it states in a sublime manner – in the absolute simplicity of a negative prescription – sublimity itself, the incommensurability of the sensible to the metaphysical.' Martin Jay has written about 'the unexpected links between the traditional iconoclastic Jewish attitude toward visual representation and a powerfully antiocular impulse in postmodernism...' in *Downcast Eyes: The Denigration of Vision in Twentieth-Century French Thought* (Berkeley, 1993).

There is a huge literature on the Jewish Abstract Expressionists which I have only sampled. James E. Breslin's *Mark Rothko* (Chicago, 1993) is very good on his subject's early life. The Tate Gallery catalogue *Mark Rothko* (London, 1999) contains the remarks of Rothko about the figurative, and the essay on the 'altar-like' character of Rothko's art (which is by Robert Rosenblum). The Newman essay is anthologized in *Abstract Expressionism*, ed. David Shapiro and Cecile Shapiro (Cambridge, 1995). Also in this anthology are Lawrence Alloway's essay on *The Stations of the Cross*, Mark Rothko's 'The Romantics were Prompted' (from which I quote), and Harold Rosenberg's 'Newman: Meaning in Abstract Art, II', from which I have taken the reference to Newman's library and which – decisively, I think – argues against regarding Newman as a Jewish artist. Gottlieb too was not a Jewish artist: he drew on themes taken from various mythologies without distinction.

Roland Doschka *Marc Chagall* (Munich, 1998) has the story about Chagall's uncle. Chagall's 'What is Jewish Art?' is in *The Golden Tradition*, ed. Lucy Dawidowicz (New York, 1984). I have taken the Liebermann story from Maria Makela *The Munich Secession* (New Jersey, 1990). The comparison of the Bomberg and El Greco pictures is made in Richard Cork *David Bomberg* (New Haven, 1987). The Boltanski remark is in Didier Semin, Tamar Garb and Donald Kuspit *Christian Boltanski* (London, 1997).

My first published attempt at understanding the complex nature of iconoclasm is the essay 'Art Crimes', *Current Legal Issues 1999* (Oxford, 1999). I distinguish two kinds of art crime: offences of reproduction, and offences of destruction. Iconoclasm is a type of the latter. (By 'art crime' I mean both crimes against art and art works which are themselves breaches of the law.) David Freedberg, perhaps the leading modern student of iconoclasm, demonstrates the continuity of iconoclastic themes in the Hebrew Scriptures and the Church Fathers, and writes about the implications of the doctrine of the Incarnation for Christian iconoclasts in *The Power of Images* (Chicago, 1989). I have taken my Eusebius and John of Damascus quotations from this book. (Such is the importance of John's argument in Christian teaching that F.H. Newman makes it over again in *An Essay on the Development of Christian Doctrine* [London, 1974; first published 1845].) Dario Gamboni *The Destruction of Art* (London, 1997) identifies iconoclastic practices in the work of 20th-century artists (I have taken the Duranty quote, and the one that immediately follows it, from this book).

The Duchamp quotations are from Gamboni, with the exception of the one about the bottle-rack, which may be found in David Joselit *Infinite Regress: Marcel Duchamp 1910–1941* (Cambridge, Mass., 1998) and the one about the *Large Glass* which is in James Hall *The World as Sculpture* (op. cit.). The comparison of *Fountain* with *The Virgin of Pimen* is made by William Camfield in 'Duchamp's *Fountain*: Aesthetic Object, Icon, or Anti-Art?', *The Definitively Unfinished Marcel Duchamp* (Cambridge, Mass., 1991), ed. Thierry De Duve. The paragraphs about Metzger are drawn from the essays by Andrew Wilson and Metzger himself in '*damaged nature, auto-destructive art*' (Nottingham, 1996). The Kiefer paragraphs are drawn from Nan Rosenthal *Anselm Kiefer: Works on Paper in the Metropolitan Museum of Art* (New York, 1998) and Lisa Saltzman *Anselm Kiefer and Art after Auschwitz* (Cambridge, 1999). I have learned a great deal from Saltzman, and I also defer to her knowledge of Kiefer's work, which is far greater than my own. I think, however, that she misreads Kiefer when she finds in his art the 'visual counterparts to Adorno's aesthetics.' Kiefer is an artist who makes art out of the materials available to him, whatever they might be. To the extent that he thinks about his art, it is as a pagan and not as a Jew. If his work does have a relation with a religious system, it is with an expansive polytheism and not with monotheism. And his work displays a fascination with Nazism which is profoundly non-Jewish. Nazism is only capable of engaging the attention of Jews when it persecutes them. But for Kiefer, its attention-demanding qualities are rather more complex, even beguiling.

I have taken my account of Byzantine iconoclasm, and the early development of Christian art, principally from a trio of books by Steven Runciman: *Byzantine Civilisation* (London, 1933), *Byzantine Style and Civilisation* (London, 1975), *The Byzantine Theocracy* (Cambridge, 1977). I am grateful to Nikos Stangos for lending me these books (and for a great deal of help and encouragement too – no author could have a better editor). Henry Chadwick *The Early Church* (London, 1967) was also very useful. The account of the emergence of Christian art given in ch. XLIX of Edward Gibbon's *The History of the Decline and Fall of the Roman Empire* (London, 1854) is, in its scepticism, inevitably sympathetic to the iconoclasts. 'The pagan rites of genuflexion, luminaries, and incense,' he comments, 'stole into the Catholic church.' It was, he says, a 'semblance of idolatry.' H.H. Milman's account, in his *History of Latin Christianity* (London, 1883), is much fuller than Gibbon's, and much less enamoured of iconoclasm, which it regards as a 'premature Rationalism, enforced upon an unreasoning age.' Unlike the iconoclasm of the Reformation, the Byzantine version 'might proscribe idolatry, but it had no power of kindling a purer faith.' Milman repeats the rumour that Leo III was inspired when young by the promises to him of two Jews that he would conquer the world if only he destroyed the images in Christendom. I do not want to overstate the historical significance of Jewish iconoclasm. Until the French Revolution, the history of art-breaking, even more than that of art-making, consists almost entirely of efforts directed by Christians against other Christians. In any event, my notion of Jewish iconoclasm has very little to do with the physical destruction of any objects – art works or otherwise.

Christians are sensitive to the charge that they violate the Second Commandment, and that they are therefore idolators. The unknown Apostolic Father who was the author of the 2nd-century 'Epistle to Diognetus' attacked both pagans and Jews for being idolators, the one for praying to idols, the other for sacrificing to Him as if He were one. 'One party ... makes its offerings to creatures which cannot partake of the gifts, and the other to One who needs none of them' (*Early Christian Writings* ed. Andrew Louth [London, 1987]). It is the Jews who are idolators, he says, not us. Their tendency to idolatry was something they picked up during their stay in Egypt.

The idolatry of the Golden Calf was typical of the Jewish mania for idols. In contrast, the faithful Gentiles have turned away from idols to the worship of the living God (see William Nicholls *Christian Antisemitism* [Northvale, N.J., 1993]). Frank E. Manuel *The Broken Staff: Judaism Through Christian Eyes* (Cambridge, Mass., 1992) demonstrates that these views were commonplace among the intelligentsia of 17th- and 18th-century Europe too.

And yet the Jews accuse us!, Christian polemicists complained. Bernard Gui, a Dominican friar writing in the early 14th century, protested that the Jews pray to God 'to cast out the graven images, that is, the images which earthly Christians adore in honour of Christ. Let the idols be destroyed...' (*Heresies of the High Middle Ages*, trans. W.L. Wakefield and A.P. Evans [New York, 1991]). There is a quite interesting passage, 'Powerful pictures', in Evelyn Welch *Art and Society in Italy 1350–1500* (Oxford, 1997), which considers the 'tensions and ambiguities in the Catholic Church's response to religious art.' It is her opinion that I quote on the treating of images as 'powerful objects'.

On the question of Christianity's debt to Classical culture (or paganism) I relied most upon Werner Jaeger's short, magisterial *Early Christianity and Greek Paideia* (Oxford, 1961). The 'old coin, new stamp' metaphor is the Jewish philosopher Philo's, as quoted by Jaeger. He writes of 'the merging of the Christian religion with the Greek intellectual heritage.' Of course, this merger took place at a number of quite different cultural levels. Jacob Burkhardt, for example, suggested both that in Italy the solidity of the popular faith depended entirely upon its pagan foundations, and that among the educated classes the worship of the saints took an essentially pagan form (*The Civilisation of the Renaissance in Italy* [London, 1951]). Donald Strong *Roman Art* (London, 1988) and Rudolf Wittkower *Allegory and the Migration of Symbols* (London, 1977) are both very good on the extent to which early Christian artists adopted pagan artistic conventions. There was, he writes, 'no fundamental conflict between Christian and pagan art: the only problem was the aesthetic one of adapting classical forms to works of the new order.' Robin Lane Fox *Pagans and Christians* (London, 1986) is my source for the information about the early Christian iconoclasm directed at pagan statuary. Neil MacGregor makes the point about the pictures in the National Gallery in his Introduction to *The Image of Christ: The Catalogue of the Exhibition 'Seeing Salvation'* (London, 2000). In the companion book, Neil MacGregor with Erika Langmuir *Seeing Salvation: Images of Christ in Art* (London, 2000), he writes: 'the life and death of Jesus Christ ... was for centuries the staple of Western

European artists ... for, with the exception of a small Jewish community, everybody in Europe would have agreed that the fact and the meaning of Christ's life and death were the most important notions that could be addressed.' Christianity, he adds, is a 'religion of the image.' It is hard, even in our present, notionally secular times, to purge the image of its religious connotations. 'The image,' asserts Jean-Luc Nancy in his essay in the exhibition catalogue *Heaven* (Ostfildern-Ruit, 1999), 'is always sacred.'

On the general question of art idolatry, the German tradition in aesthetics is examined most usefully in Andrew Bowie *Aesthetics and Subjectivity* (Manchester, 1990) and J.M. Bernstein *The Fate of Art* (Cambridge, 1992). The 'aesthetic alibi' arguments are to be found in Martin Jay *Cultural Semantics* (Amherst, 1998) and George Orwell 'Benefit of Clergy: Some Notes on Salvador Dali' in *Collected Essays, Journalism and Letters 3* (London, 1970). Both Jay and Orwell are critical of the alibi, and indeed Orwell argues that it should be possible to say: 'This is a good book or a good picture, and it ought to be burned by the public hangman.' Roger Shattuck, in *Candor and Perversion: Literature, Education and the Arts* (New York, 1999), deprecates the use of the alibi to 'protect and ennoble displays of unredeemed depravity and violence.'

In the first draft of this book, I developed the argument about connoisseurship in relation to the career of Bernard Berenson. When he was a young man, he says, he approached a work of art with what he describes as 'reverent receptivity'. He would go on 'pilgrimage after pilgrimage' to see a picture in some remote church. On the way, he would get into a state of grace towards the picture; on leaving, he would be filled with its image. (This anecdote comes from his edited diaries, *The Passionate Sightseer* [London, 1960].) Such a person could have no sympathy for the Jewish tradition. And his observations on the Jews and the visual arts – essentially, that there is no Jewish art, mainly because Jews are no good at art – confirm this intuition. See his *Aesthetics and History* (London, 1950), in which he writes of 'the fanatical hatred of the anti-Hellenic Jew against everything that might entice him away from his bleak abstractions and the passionately fervid, aggressive, and exasperated affirmation of his monotheism.' Herbert Read's similar argument, which I mention in the main text, is made in *The Meaning of Art* (London, 1931). The book remained in print right into the 1970s. It was against opinions of this kind that Jewish historians struggled. See, for example, S.W. Baron's *A Social and Religious History of the Jews*, Vol. 1, 2nd ed. (New York, 1952): 'It was no lack of artistic ability which prevented the Jews from creating plastic representations of their deity.... Conscious restraint rather than native inability appears to have been the determining factor.'

On Bruskin, there are two catalogues that I have been able to consult, both published by Marlborough Galleries, one in 1990 and the other in 1994. The critics who see no difficulty in Bruskin's 'Book' metaphor are Yevgeni Barabanov and Christopher Sweet, whose essays preface the 1990 and 1994 catalogues respectively. The Baigells also interviewed him in their *Soviet Dissident Artists* (op. cit.), and the reference to idols comes from this source. Relating Soviet ideology to an iconostasis was prompted by Otto Karl Werckmeister *Icons of the Left* (Chicago, 1999). The notion of the idolatry of the text is developed in Marc-Alain Ouaknin *The Burnt Book* (Princeton, 1995): 'the Text should be elusive, impregnable, and should never take on the form of an idol. The Cabalists explain that the Text, the Torah, and God are one.... The relationship with the Text and with God is paradoxical: one must move away, create a distance, if the relation with God is not going to be idolatrous.'

LIST OF ILLUSTRATIONS

The publishers would like to thank the following for their advice and help in the preparation of the illustrations: Jean Adams, Denora Davies-Rees, Graham Ward, Breck Hostetter, Vitaly Komar and Alexander Melamid, Joshua Neustein, Galerie Onrust. Please note that while every effort has been made to trace all the copyright holders of the works included in this book, the publishers would be grateful to be notified of any omissions so that these may be included in any reprint.

Measurements are given in centimetres followed by inches, height before width.

1 Jean-Auguste-Dominique Ingres, *The Vow of Louis XIII*, 1824. Oil on canvas, 421 x 261.9 (165 3/4 x 103 1/8) Cathedral, Montauban/Photo: Bulloz

2 Komar and Melamid, *The Origins of Socialist Realism*, 1982–83. Oil on canvas, 183 x 122 (72 x 48). Collection of Ronald and Frayda Feldman. Courtesy Ronald Feldman Fine Arts, New York. Photo: D. James Dee.

3 Jean-Auguste-Dominique Ingres, *Napoleon I on his Imperial Throne*, 1806. Oil on canvas, 265.7 x 160 (104 5/8 x 63). Musée de l'Armée, Palais des Invalides, Paris/Photo: Giraudon

4 Jean-Auguste-Dominique Ingres, *Jupiter and Thetis*, 1811. Oil on canvas, 347 x 257.2 (136 5/8 x 101 1/4). Musée Granet, Aix-en-Provence/ Photo: Giraudon

5 Raphael, *Crucifixion with Two Angels, the Virgin and Three Saints (the Mond Crucifixion)*, 1503–4. Oil on panel, 280 x 165 (110 1/4 x 65). National Gallery, London

6 Fra Bartolommeo, *Vision of Saint Bernard*, 1504–7. Oil on canvas, 220 x 213 (86 5/8 x 83 7/8). Galleria Palatina, Palazzo Pitti, Florence/ Photo: Scala

7 Raphael, *Madonna and Child with Saint John (Madonna della Sedia)*, 1513. Oil on panel, diameter 71 (28). Galleria Palatina, Palazzo Pitti, Florence

8 Raphael, *Adoration of the Golden Calf*, ninth vault from frescoes of the Vatican Loggias, 1516–19. Palazzi Vaticani, Rome

9 David Allan, *The Origin of Painting*, 1775. Oil on wood, 76.2 x 63.5 (30 x 25). National Galleries of Scotland, Edinburgh/Photo: Annan

10 Luca Cambiaso, *Madonna and Child*, *c.* 1565, 208.3 x 170.2 (82 x 67). Mauritshuis, The Hague

11 Mikhail Roshal, *We Shall Mine Extra Coal*, 1973. Tempera, board, primer on board, 80 x 60 (31 1/2 x 23 5/8). Property of the Artist. Photo: Valentin Chertok

12 Komar and Melamid, *Double Self-Portrait as Young Pioneers*, 1983. Oil on canvas 182.9 x 127 (72 x 50). Private Collection. Courtesy of Ronald Feldman Fine Arts, New York/ Photo: D. James Dee

13 Feodor Shurpin, *The Morning of Our Fatherland*, 1948. Iskusttvo/© DACS 2001

14 Sergei Merkurov, *Statue of Stalin*, 1940s

15 Otto Hoyer, *In the Beginning Was the Word*, 1937. Department of Defense, Washington D.C.

16 *The Crucifixion and Iconoclasts* from the Chludov Psalter (folio 67r), mid-ninth century CE. Illuminated manuscript. State Historical Museum, Moscow

17 Masaccio, *The Trinity*, *c.* 1427, fresco. Santa Maria Novella, Florence/ Photo: Scala

18 Kazimir Malevich, *Black Square*, 1915. Oil on canvas, 106.2 x 106.5 ($41\frac{3}{4}$ x $41\frac{7}{8}$). State Tretyakov Gallery, Moscow

19 '0.10' exhibition, Petrograd, 1915. Photograph: Klaus Hurrgimalla, Frankfurt

20 Mark Rothko, *Untitled*, 1951. Oil on canvas 237.5 x 144.1 ($93\frac{1}{2}$ x $56\frac{3}{4}$). Los Angeles County Museum of Art, Exposition Park. Collection: Mr and Mrs Gifford Phillips, Washington D.C. © Kate Rothko Prizel & Christopher Rothko/DACS, 2001

21 Alain Kirili, *Commandment II*, 1980. The Jewish Museum, NY/Art Resource, NY

22 Eli Content, *Untitled*, 1986–87. Oil on canvas 160 x 160 (63 x 63). Courtesy of Galerie Onrust, Amsterdam

23 Joshua Neustein, *To Stella*, 1973–77. Drawing (torn paper), 250 x 195 ($98\frac{3}{8}$ x $76\frac{3}{4}$). Collection of the Artist

24 Max Weber, *Adoration of the Moon*, 1944. Whitney Museum of American Art

25 Ben Shahn, *Sound in the Mulberry Trees*, 1948. Smith College Museum of Art/© Estate of Ben Shahn/VAGA, New York/DACS, London 2001

26 Max Liebermann, *Jesus in the Temple*, 1879. Oil on canvas, 151 x 131 ($59\frac{1}{2}$ x $51\frac{5}{8}$). Private Collection, on loan to the Hamburger Kunsthalle/© DACS 2001

27 David Bomberg, *Hear O Israel*, 1955. Oil on canvas, 91.5 x 71 (36 x 28). © The Family of the Artist

28 El Greco, *Christ Carrying the Cross*, 1590–95. Oil on canvas 108 x 78 ($42\frac{1}{2}$ x $30\frac{3}{4}$). Museo del Prado, Madrid

29 Anatolii Brussilovsky, *Two Ideas*, 1984. Collage, 45.7 x 50.8 (18 x 20)

30 Marc Chagall, *Resistance*, 1937–48. Oil on canvas, 168 x 104.1 ($66\frac{1}{8}$ x 41). Musée National Message Biblique Marc Chagall, Nice/Photo: Philippe Migeat, Centre Georges Pompidou, Paris/© ADAGP, Paris and DACS, London 2001

31 Marc Chagall, *Resurrection*, 1937–48. Oil on canvas 165.4 x 105.1 ($65\frac{1}{8}$ x $41\frac{3}{8}$). Musée National Message Biblique Marc Chagall, Nice/Photo: Philippe Migeat, Centre Georges Pompidou, Paris/© ADAGP, Paris and DACS, London 2001

32 Marc Chagall, *Liberation*, 1937–52. Oil on canvas, 168 x 87.9 ($66\frac{1}{8}$ x $34\frac{5}{8}$). Musée National Message Biblique Marc Chagall, Nice/Photo:

David Vence/© ADAGP, Paris and DACS, London 2001

33 Maryan S. Maryan, *Personage with Donkey Ears*, 1962. Oil on canvas 127 x 127 (50 x 50). Photo courtesy of George Adams Gallery, New York

34 Ferdinand Staeger, *SS on Guard*, n.d. Oil on canvas. Zeitungsmagazin, Hamburg

35 Rudolf Otto, *Ready for Battle*, n.d. Oil on canvas. Oberfinanzdirektion, Munich

36 Mikhail Shvartsman, *Space of the Trinity*, 1986. Oil on board, 100 x 100 (39 3/8 x 39 3/8). The artist.

37 Aleksei Sundokov, *Prolonged and Undiminished Applause*, 1987. Oil on canvas, 150 x 200 (50 x 78 3/4). The artist.

38 Simen Faibisovich, *Before Bathing*, 1988. Oil on canvas, 150 x 200 (59 x 78 3/4). The artist.

39 Mikhail Grobman, *Our Power is in Zionism*, 1996. Photograph 76.2 x 111.8 (30 x 44)

40 Komar and Melamid, from 'Monumental Propaganda': Statue of Felix Dzerzhinsky (detail), 1993. Computer graphic, 27.9 x 21.6 (11 x 8 1/2)

41 Komar and Melamid, from 'Monumental Propaganda': Statue of Karl Marx (detail), 1993. Computer graphic, 27.9 x 21.6 (11 x 8 1/2)

42 Vera Mukhina, *Worker and Peasant*, 1937

43 Art Spiegelman, *One Step Forward, Two Steps Back (After)*, 1992. Colour photocopy, 27.9 x 21.6 (11 x 8 1/2)

44 Komar and Melamid, *America's Most Wanted*, 1994. Oil and acrylic on canvas, 61 x 81.3 (24 x 32)/dishwasher-size. Courtesy of Ronald Feldman Fine Arts, New York/Photo: D. James Dee

45 Komar and Melamid, *America's Most Unwanted*, 1994. Tempera and oil on canvas, 14 x 21.6 (5 1/2 x 8 1/2)/paperback book-size. Courtesy of Ronald Feldman Fine Arts, New York/Photo: D. James Dee

46 Komar and Melamid, *Kenya's Most Wanted*, 1996. Oil on canvas, 40.6 x 66 (16 x 26). Courtesy of the artists

47 Komar and Melamid, *Kenya's Most Unwanted*, 1996. Mixed media on wood, 14 x 20.3 (5 1/2 x 8). Courtesy of the artists

48 Komar and Melamid, *Iceland's Most Unwanted*, 1995. Acrylic on wood 14 x 21.6 (5 1/2 x 8 1/2). Courtesy of the artists

49 Komar and Melamid, *Iceland's Most Wanted*, 1995. Oil on canvas 66 x 96.5 (26 x 38). Courtesy of the artists

50 From *The Pennysaver*, Ithaca, New York, 19–26 October 1994

51 Komar and Melamid, *Post Art No. 1 (Warhol)*, 1973. Courtesy of the artists

52 Marcel Duchamp, *L.H.O.O.Q.*, 1919. Rectified readymade: pencil on reproduction, 19.7 x 12.4 (7 3/4 x 4 7/8). Private Collection, Paris/© Succession Marcel Duchamp/ADAGP, Paris and DACS, London 2001

53 Alfred Stieglitz, photo of Marcel Duchamp's *Fountain* (cropped), 1917. 10.8 x 17.8 (4 1/4 x 7). Philadelphia Museum of Art; The Louise and Walter Arensberg Collection

54 Gustav Metzger, *South Bank Demonstration*, 3 July 1961. Photo: Hulton Getty

55 Anselm Kiefer, *Saint Eustace*, 1974. Watercolour, gouache and coloured pencil on paper, 20.6 x 27.3 (8 $\frac{1}{8}$ x 10 $\frac{3}{4}$). The Metropolitan Museum of Art, New York. Promised gift of Cynthia Hazen Polsky, in memory of her father, Joseph H. Hazen. By permission of the artist

56 Albrecht Dürer, *Saint Eustace* (detail), *c.* 1500–1. Engraving. The Metropolitan Museum of Art, New York, Fletcher Fund, 1919

57 Anselm Kiefer, *Herzeleide*, 1979. Watercolour, gouache and graphite pencil on paper, 47.6 x 35.9 (18 $\frac{3}{4}$ x 14 $\frac{1}{8}$). The Metropolitan Museum of Art, New York. Purchase, Lila Acheson Wallace Gift, 1995. By permission of the artist

58 Anselm Kiefer, *Every Man Stands Beneath His Own Dome of Heaven*, 1970. Watercolour, gouache, and graphite pencil on joined paper, 40 x 47.9 (15 $\frac{3}{4}$ x 18 $\frac{7}{8}$). The Metropolitan Museum of Art, New York. Denise and Andrew Saul Fund, 1995, 1995.14.4. By permission of the artist

59 Anselm Kiefer, *Iconoclastic Controversy*, 1980. Gouache and pen and ink on photograph, 50.2 x 80 (19 $\frac{3}{4}$ x 31 $\frac{1}{2}$). The Metropolitan Museum of Art, New York. Purchase, Lila Acheson Wallace Gift, 1995. By permission of the artist

60 Members of Hitler Youth burning books, Berlin 1933. Photograph: Hulton Getty

61 Garvens, 'The Sculptor of Germany', from *Jugend*, 1933

62 Grisha Bruskin, *Alephbet–Lexicon 7*, 1990. Oil on linen, 119.4 x 91.4 (47 x 36). Copyright Grisha Bruskin; courtesy Marlborough Gallery, New York

63 Grisha Bruskin, *Message 3*, 1989–90. Oil on linen, 140 x 112 (55 $\frac{1}{8}$ x 44 $\frac{1}{8}$). Copyright Grisha Bruskin; courtesy Marlborough Gallery, New York

64 Grisha Bruskin, *Partner*, 1978. Oil on linen 99.1 x 81.3 (39 x 32). Copyright Grisha Bruskin, courtesy Marlborough Gallery, New York

65 Jacob Kramer, *Day of Atonement*, 1919. Oil on canvas 99.6 x 122.4 (39 $\frac{1}{4}$ x 48 $\frac{1}{4}$). Leeds City Art Gallery

66 Itzhak Danziger, *Nimrod*, 1939. Nubian sandstone, 100 x 33 (39 $\frac{3}{8}$ x 13). Photo: I. Zafrir, Tel Aviv